# igloo

Published in 2011
by Igloo Books Ltd
Cottage Farm
Sywell
NN6 OBJ

www.igloo-books.com

Copyright © 2011 Igloo Books Ltd

L006 1111

10 9 8 7 6 5 4 3 2 1

ISBN: 978-0-85780-242-2

Printed and manufactured in China

# 101

# 101 WAYS TO SAY I Love You

igloo

# CONTENTS

# GETAWAYS

# ZERO COST

# OUTSIDE THE BOX

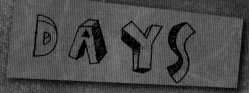

BUCKET AND spade DAYS

# SAY IT IN SAND

Remember those old bucket and spade days of childhood, down on the beach drawing lines in the sand? Now you have a great excuse to do it again and make your loved one smile into the bargain.

Find yourself a nice empty stretch of sandy beach. Then write the words I Love You and their name in huge letters in the sand. Enlist a friendly local and get them to take a photograph of you next to the giant words.

Next, print it off and frame it for your loved one. If they have a job, then surprise them and post it to their place of work. If they're at home then hide it somewhere and leave them directions to the hiding place, like a treasure hunt.

The picture is sure to bring a big smile to their face! If you want to make it even more special you could use the picture as a hint to what you're planning in the future. If you fancy a day trip or a week away at the seaside, send the picture and then reveal your plans for a bucket and spade break.

Even better, if you're planning to go abroad, then write I love you in the language of the country. Here are a few to get you started:
Spanish: Te Amo
French: Je t'aime
Italian: Ti Amo

If you live too far away from the beach, don't worry. If you have children with a sandpit or know somebody who has one in their garden, write it in that!

# GREEN GRASS OF LOVE

**M**ow it into the lawn or do it with cress! You don't have to be a professional to use your garden to get romantic. If you have a lawn, you can do it with that. Depending on the size of the lawn, you can choose to write the words, mow a heart, spell their name or intertwine your initials for extra impact.

First, let the grass grow quite long. If you're a bit of a perfectionist, you may find the tall grass annoys you a bit, but remember it's for a purpose. Choose a day to mow the grass when they are out. Make sure you systematically spell out the words or initials and clear up the clippings afterwards for real effect.

If you want to make it even more striking, then lay a trail of paper arrows with hearts on them all the way from the front door to the back door and out into the garden. If you don't have a lawn or only have a small patch of grass, you can use cress instead. For this one you need to plan ahead as cress takes seven to 10 days to grow.

Place several sheets of good quality kitchen paper on a tray and dampen with cold water. Sprinkle a packet of cress seeds in the shape of a heart or their name or initial. Place the tray on a window ledge somewhere that they are unlikely to look and leave it to grow. Remember to make sure the kitchen paper stays nice and damp in order for the seeds to germinate. Once it has grown, present it to them.

# RHYME TIME

One of the most time-honoured ways to say I love you. You don't have to be William Shakespeare to pen a poem. Even if you think your creative skills don't stretch that far, you'll be surprised. Be as deep and intimate as you like, making your poem light and fluffy or silly and funny. It really doesn't matter what you come up with, so long as it's about them.

If you're feeling stumped, think about all the things you like about them. The way their hair curls on their neck or the funny way they eat chips. You could use the time you first met as a starting point, or write something about their favourite things.

Remember that poems don't have to rhyme! One of the easiest forms to try is the Haiku, a Japanese poem of three lines, with 5-7-5 syllables.

For example:

Rosie, the light falls

On your gorgeous curls, making

Me yearn to kiss you.

The key thing about poetry is that it's personal. Tell them why you love them, it could be something as simple as you love the way they laugh at your jokes, even when they're not funny.

Make sure that you handwrite whatever you come up with, it's much more personal. Choose thick creamy paper and invest in a quality pen. Calligraphy pens aren't expensive and the end result will look stunning.

# MAGNETIC ATTRACTION

**V**isit a toy shop and buy yourself a great big box of alphabet magnets, then have a field day on all your magnetic surfaces. If you are last in bed and they are first up in the morning, get to work before the lights go out. Spell out a love note in these brightly coloured letters on the refrigerator.

If you know they will be using the washing machine or dryer, then you could leave an array of love words on the doors. Some stores even sell packs of magnetic words so you can create whole sentences telling your partner just what they mean to you. The big benefit of this one is that it gives them a chance to say something nice back as they can jumble up the letters and start all over again.

You'd be surprised just how many magnetic surfaces there are around the house but it's safe to stick to the usual ones like the refrigerator, washing machine and dryer. If you don't have much space on yours for love messages, then invest in a big bag of foam letters instead.

These are great for sticking on to tiled surfaces, like the bath or shower. Simply wet the walls and stick them on in the order of things you want to say. Foam letters are a great option as they leave no mess and don't require anything to stick them on.

If you've got children, you could borrow their Lego and other building bricks and spell out your love for your partner that way.

# PEN TO PAPER

**W**e've got out of the habit of writing down how we feel and this is a beautiful and lasting way to do it. Think back to the older generations. When they were apart there was no telephone or email so the only way of keeping in touch was by letter.

You can really say how you feel in a letter and the very idea that someone has sat down and really thought about what to say can make all the difference and raise wonderful sentiments. Be as slushy or as straightforward as you like.

Your romance is unique and what you share with your partner is completely different from everyone else. Tell them how you feel, tell them what you're up to and make them laugh. Couples have their own language and shared experiences, use that to make your letter as personal as possible.

Pick your paper carefully. You could just use A4 printer paper or buy some proper letter-writing paper. Spray it with a dash of your eau de toilette scent so that when they open the letter, your familiar aroma will burst from the page.

Make sure you write by hand. It can be hard work in these days of computers, but it makes all the difference. Be careful as you fold the letter, making sure you do it neatly and slot it into the envelope carefully. Don't forget the postage stamp, a little cash spent is worth it!

Take it to the mail box yourself and give the letter a kiss before you post it for extra luck in love! Imagine their surprise when they open and read it!

# FLOWER LETTERS

You can buy a bunch of their favourite flowers, but that's predictable and quite ordinary in terms of telling them you love them. How about spelling it out with flowers instead? If you're worried about buying fresh flowers to do this and then finding them all droopy and dying, then go to a craft store and buy silk flowers instead.

There are two ways to spell out your love in flowers: on a flat surface or in a series of vases along the counter in the kitchen. Decide what you want to say. It could be their name, the day of your first date or a simple 'I Love You.'

For extra effect, choose flowers in their favourite color. Or if they have a favourite flower, choose that. If they love roses, buy them in graduating shades of pink for a real crescendo effect. Or if carnations are their thing, choose a rainbow of colors.

If you're using fresh flowers, get your vases together and fill them with water. Then bend the flowers carefully into the shape of the letters and put them in a line. You can easily improvise on some letters, by adding colorful drinking straws for a truly artistic arrangement.

If you're using silk or paper flowers, you can use any flat surface. If you want to surprise them when they get home, arrange them on the doormat. Or, spell out your love step by step, so that when they climb upstairs, their journey will tell them just what they mean to you!

# STEAMY MESSAGES

If you're the first one to use the shower in the morning, make sure you leave it nice and tidy for them and why not remind them of your love by leaving a message on the fogged up mirror. A hot shower means condensation, so leave a love note on the mirror or window where they are sure to see it.

You can do this in many locations. If they've been cooking dinner and the kitchen windows get all steamy, write a thank you note on the glass to remind them how much you love them. Who knows, it might lead to a different kind of steamy later on!

Use variations of this idea, depending on where you are. If you travel home by bus together, then try getting on a stop before they do. Grab a window seat and draw a heart in the fog, then as the bus stops, wave at them through the heart.

If you're on a train together, wait until it goes into a tunnel and then breathe on the darkened window. Tell them you love them by writing a note on the steamed up part and it will show up like magic once you're out of the tunnel.

When summer turns to autumn, cars tend to get fogged up in the mornings. Leave for work before them and tell them you love them on the windscreen, it's sure to bring a smile to their face on a dull morning.

If you want to do something more lasting there are other things you can use, for example, spray your heart's desires on to the mirror using shaving foam in the bathroom. Or, if you get out of a bubbly bath and there are still loads of bubbles left over, use them to create a heart on the tiles to make them smile!

# SWEET LOVE NOTES

Has your life become so busy that you feel like you rarely bump into your partner, even though you live in the same house? Then invest in post-it notes and get scribbling. These sticky-backed bits of paper are a godsend when it comes to keeping in touch. The advantage of the adhesive means they stay put, so there are no worries about a gust of wind carting off a well-thought out note out of the window.

Don't always choose the most expected locations for your notes, try leaving them somewhere extraordinary. If they wake up before you, stick a note on their mug. If they always have cornflakes for breakfast, leave a note inside the box for them to find.

But don't just stick to home ground. Stick a post-it on their cell phone, in their jacket pocket, or leave a loved-up message on their laptop. Notes work well for all kinds of friendships. You don't need to be lovers to like to receive a note. Post-it notes are great for showing people you care.

They are readily available in all shapes and sizes and plenty of different colours. You can even buy heart-shaped ones to emphasise just how you feel about your mate. You could even make a post-it pact where each of you has a stack of different coloured notes and see who can come up with the most original place to leave a note. You could celebrate the winner with a glass of wine or a simple cup of coffee!

## LOVE SPEAKS OUT

If all you get on your voicemail are messages from work colleagues or vendors, then this one works well. It's also good for people who rarely use their cell phone as it brings a great element of surprise.

Choose a time when you know they won't be able to answer their phone. Before you call, work out what you want to say. Plan to leave a sequence of messages over a period of time. That way, when they think they have got three messages and reluctantly play them back expecting boring messages, they'll be surprised to hear your voice.

The messages don't need to be long. As the saying goes: it's the thought that counts. You can just leave a message that says 'I'm thinking of you.' Save the longer conversations for when you're back together face to face.

And never leave messages that say 'call me.' There's nothing worse than receiving a message without giving them any idea of why you want them to call you. If you leave a message like that they're bound to think something that something has gone wrong.

If you leave telephone messages at their workplace, make sure you don't say anything too sexy or saucy, think how embarrassing it would be if they were on speaker phone when they played your message.

If you're saying something for their ears only, make sure you keep it clean and cryptic rather than blurting out something that would embarrass them if anyone else were to hear it!

# GET IN FIRST

This one needs careful timing. Do they go out to work at the same time every day? If they do, this is an easy one to do. Keep track of when they leave and double check with them what time they start work.

Then the moment they've left the house, get scribbling. The aim is to send them a lovely email so that when they turn on their computer at work, the first email in their inbox will be from you. Knowing a loved one is thinking about you moments after you have left for work is going to give them a nice warm and fuzzy feeling.

If your loved one doesn't have access to a computer at work then email their home account just before they leave work so that your message will be one of the first messages they see when they get home in the evening.

What to say? Whatever you like. It could be a great way to say thanks for a lovely evening or maybe you know they have something on their mind that's bothering them. Send them a reassuring message, reminding them that you are thinking about them and can't wait to see them when you get home.

It's a great feeling to open your inbox and to see a really personal message in amongst all those boring emails that demand your attention and take up so much of your time.

make

texting

more

romantic

# CHARMING TEXTS

It may sound obvious in this day and age, but ask around and you'll be surprised to find that many couples and long term lovers rarely text message their feelings. We've all done it and it's so easy to get into the habit of using text messaging for factual stuff and forgetting the meaningful bits.

Why not promise yourself a week to make text messaging more romantic? Forget those missives that say 'please buy milk on your way home' and rekindle the romance in your soul.

You can make this more fun by agreeing to send each other a certain number of text messages a day. For example, if you decide to send six texts then spread them out through the day like little meals of love, sustenance to keep them going through the daily grind.

The main thing is to send enough text messages and not too many. If you send dozens it can quite simply get annoying and it makes it impossible for anyone busy at work to respond to them.

If your partner is away or if you don't live together yet, then send them a good morning or a goodnight text message. This also works really well if you work different hours and don't see each other in the same way as people with ordinary nine to five jobs.

Maybe your loved one is a long distance courier driver, why not send them a text when they're settling down for the night before an early start on the road. Or, perhaps they work in a hospital through the night, coming home bleary eyed and ready for bed when you're starting work. Cheer them up by sending them a cheery goodnight text they'll cherish forever!

**CARD ROMANCE**

If you don't feel like writing a letter then choose a card and remember to post it for best effect. A card is a great way to remind them how much they mean to you and there are thousands of different types of cards out there. The tip is to take time choosing the right one.

Pick a card that sums up how you feel about things right now. If things are going great, then choose something happy, smiley and cheerful. If they have specific hobbies then try to reflect that. For instance, if they're keen on golf, pick an appropriate card and try and make your words fit the picture. How about: 'you'll be on my fairway forever!'

Country scenes can sum up the peace you feel in your relationship. Or maybe you both feel the need for a few nights away but money is tight. Send them a card with a picture of an idyllic location and tell them you wish you could whisk them away to it. Suggest they keep it as a memento until you can afford to make it a reality.

Choose funny cards if someone is down, it's a great way to cheer them up. If you're feeling inventive you could choose a sequence of cards and send one every few days. This works really well if you are building up to an event, such as proposing marriage or going on holiday. Send a few cards over a few days to build up the excitement. Try to remain cryptic though, you don't have to write much in a card, just enough to be intriguing!

# HAPPY SERENADE

k, so you may not be the next Céline Dion or Frank Sinatra, but have a go anyway. You don't have to come up with the lyrics, unless you want to, just find a song you know they love.

You can print off the words from many Internet sites and while they are out, practise it until you're literally word perfect. One of the best places to perfect your song is in the car while you are driving. That way, no one can hear you crunch the notes or fluff the lines.

Pick your perfect moment to play pop diva, making sure you're both relaxed in really good humour. Grab them by the hand, flick on your MP3 player or pop a CD into the slot and begin your debut.

You never know where it will lead, they might even join in and before you know it you'll be singing a duet! If you're feeling adventurous, you can adapt a song to make it more personal.

To do this you will need more time and thought to get the lines to flow perfectly. Try adding some things that make the person super-special to you. Once you've tried adapting a song for your loved one, then you really will be ready to write your own!

If it's easier, you can set it to a tune you are already familiar with and then simply let rip with your feelings. Include details of things you like about them and if you make it funny too, then you're on the right track to winning their heart.

# GET PERSONAL

Even though this may seem a little old-fashioned, this is a sure-fire way of reaffirming your love. Why not place a message in the personal ads of your local newspaper? Some national newspapers and magazines also have personal ad sections, so go right ahead.

Years ago, the personal column was where people kept in touch, where people who had lost contact tried to find each other and where messages about lost dogs were aired. In those days, with no email or cell phones it was seen as a real lifeline.

Nowadays, you pay by the word for the personal ads in newspapers so work out carefully how much you have to spend and just what you want to say. You could be straightforward and use their name and yours. Or, why not get cryptic and use one of your pet names, if you have them for each other?

This can be even more surprising if they don't usually read the newspaper where you've chosen to place your ad. Once you've placed the ad, keep a note of the date it will be printed. Imagine the confusion on their face when you suggest they read the paper. You could pretend to point out something interesting on the page and then watch their eyes wander as they spot their very own personal message!

# TRUMPET your love

# SPORT YOUR LOVE

**M**ake your love truly public by saying it at a football game. Most grounds with electronic scoreboards are more than happy to take your requests and trumpet your love to everyone else at the game.

You need to be able to keep it short and sweet and if your partner is a big sports fan, they'll be delighted to see their name and very own personal message flash up on the scoreboard.

Combine the declaration of your love with a trip to a game. Either go with them, or if they go with their friends, send them a text message before the interval, telling them to keep their eyes peeled. In fact, this is one that works just as well whether you are there or not.

If you're at the game, watch their face light up as your dedication flashes up on the screen. If you're not with them, expect a text message or call expressing their surprise.

If you go for this idea, make sure you plan well ahead. Bigger clubs get lots of requests just like this, so it's best to get in early to be in with a chance of it being shown.

You could also adapt this idea to other public places, for instance, the local bowling alley. Call them in advance and ask if they will display your declaration of love on the scoreboard, you could time it perfectly so that it flashes up when your loved one scores their very own strike!

If you don't attend many sport events and prefer, instead, to watch it from the comfort of your own home, then make your own scoreboard, including your declaration and pin it to the wall during the game.

cute way to pass the time when you're at home or in the car. You can make these as sensible or as saucy as you like. If you're feeling romantic, play I Spy and pick all the things that you like about your lover. It can certainly spice up an evening. Keep a score of who's winning, with the proviso that the loser cooks dinner.

Use your imagination by playing the shopping game. Start with the letter A and work through the alphabet, outlining all the things you'd buy them if you had unlimited amounts of money. You could start with an imaginary Aston Martin, move on to diamonds, right through to a villa. Then get them to do the same for you.

Adapt old-fashioned games to suit your love life. Ask your partner to come up with 10 things they love about you in one minute. For every one they can't think of, give them a forfeit, exactly what kind of forfeit will be up to you!

Play hangman. Think of a word that means a lot to you and see if your partner can guess it. If they end up getting 'hanged' because they couldn't think of it, then give them a crash course in learning more about you.

Sign up to a session of noughts and crosses, with rewards for the first person to get to five. All these childhood games take on that extra frisson when they're played with you lover.

Spice up an evening

include

THEIR

dreams

# CREATIVE CHARM

Cut out pictures and headlines from newspapers and magazines that sum up everything your loved one means to you. Make sure you include every little thing you can think of about them.

Find pictures of the food they like, whether it's pizza or caviar. Include pictures of the car they drive and the car they would have if they won the lottery!

Include their dreams in there, even if they seem impossible. If their ambition is to cross the equator, then include a picture of a globe. If one day they want to climb a mountain, pick a shot of a snowy peak. If they have a favorite color, try and choose pictures that reflect that.

If you want to use the collage as a hint to a gift, then stick words across the pictures that provide clues. For instance if you've bought them tickets to a concert, cut out the date, time and place where it's happening. If you're taking them out for a meal, include the name of the restaurant.

Next, take a large piece of paper and cardboard and cut out the words I Love You from a magazine. Start by placing that in the middle of the cardboard and fill in the edges with all the pictures and words. As you build up the collage you'll be amazed at how good it looks and will fall that little bit more in love with them.

This is an inexpensive way of showing someone how much you really care and also shows how much thought and effort you have put in to make their gift extra-special.

# Ways to Say I Love You...

## FOOD

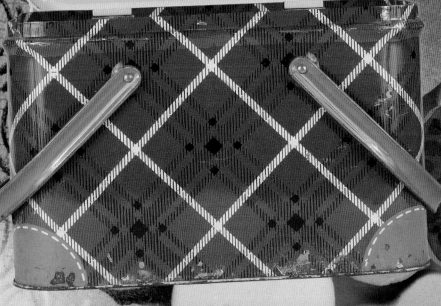

# GET TOASTING

This is one of the easiest ways to liven up someone's morning. You can tailor make this idea to any food you like, so if your loved one adores bananas you can create a heart-shaped banana in the centre of the bread.

First of all, take a sheet of paper the size of a slice of bread and cut out a heart shape. Place a couple of slices of bread in the toaster or under a grill. When they're toasted pop them onto a plate.

Then, pick your topping, or rather their favorite topping. It could be bananas, honey, cheese or even peanut butter. Using your template as a guide spread the topping so that a heart shape is created. If the template gets a bit messy, don't worry, it's only paper and you can easily make another one.

If you don't want to do hearts, the world is your oyster. You can cut out initials, or use a circle to signify a hug, or make an x shape to signify a big kiss on the toast.

If you fancy doing something different with the toast then do it the other way round. Toast the bread in the usual way but instead of using a cut out to create a shape, cut out the shape in the bread instead.

The world is your OYSTER

Spell out your adoration

# PIZZA PASSION

If you have a day when you don't have time to cook, order their favorite pizza instead , but make sure it's their favorite, not yours. That means if they adore anchovies and pineapple then you'll just have to deal with it for love!

Then take a sheet of greaseproof paper and write I Love You on it. Make sure you answer the door when the pizza arrives and slip the note underneath the pizza. When they takes a slice or two your message will become clear!

If you want to get creative yourself then make your own pizza. Buy some ready made pizza bases, smear them with tomato purée and sprinkle with mozzarella cheese. Then spell out your adoration in toppings. Either create a heart shape (sliced peppers are good for this) or make them a loving smiley face with pepperoni for eyes, sliced tomato for a nose and a grinning row of chopped bacon for a really happy meal.

You could also spell out their name or initial using toppings. Or, why not try making mini pizzas, each one with a letter of their name on top. If they have a long name, it can mean a lot of little pizzas, but romance is hungry work and pizza makes a fine cold snack the day after.

For a really caring pizza treat, make a pizza entirely of their favourite toppings. If you're with someone whose idea of heaven is a pizza topped with anchovies, olives and pineapple, then go right ahead. They'll be absolutely thrilled when they see what you've done  and may even return the favor next time!

# SPAGHETTI TIME

Spaghetti and meatballs can be one of the most romantic meals on the planet, so long as you don't mind the risk of getting covered in a spot of tomato sauce. Remember the wonderful Disney film Lady and the Tramp? The Italian waiter serenades the loved-up dogs over spaghetti and meatballs.

Both Lady and Tramp are so preoccupied with the food and the music that they don't notice that each of them has picked the opposite end of the same piece of spaghetti. Of course, their lips meet in the middle in what has to be one of the sweetest, most romantic scenes of any Disney movie.

To recreate your own scene, set the table so your places are close together. Next, create some perfect meatballs in rich tomato sauce and cook the spaghetti to go with it. Pile it all up on one large plate. Put on some soft romantic music and tuck in. Make sure you leave the spaghetti nice and long for maximum laughs and love interest.

Of course, if you want to recreate the scene exactly, you could eat the spaghetti outside under the stars and then when you've finished, take a moonlit walk to the park where you'll see that even the ducks have their mates!

If you don't fancy the Italian influence, dig out the wok, get some spicy hoisin sauce and a bag of twisty noodles. This can be even more fun as you try and catch the same long noodle with a pair of chopsticks.

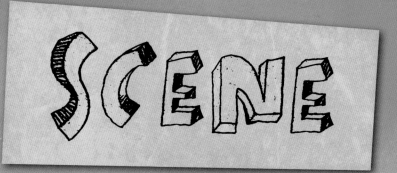

Everyone

LOVES

# CUTE CUPCAKES

Everyone loves a cake and cupcakes can be personalised so easily that it's worth putting some effort in for your loved one. Rustle up some cute cupcakes using this easy recipe and have fun decorating them.

Ingredients:

- 125 g / 4.5 oz / 1 1/4 cups butter, softened
- 125 g / 4.5 oz / 1 1/4 cups caster sugar
- 2 large eggs
- 175 g / 6 oz / 1 3/4 cup self-raising flour
- Vanilla essence
- A few drops of milk, if needed

Method:
Mix the butter and sugar together in a bowl until soft and creamy. Whisk the eggs and stir lightly into the mixture. Add a couple of drops of vanilla essence and gradually fold in the flour. Add a few drops of milk if the mixture seems too stiff. Next, line a cup cake tin with cake cases. Add a dessert-spoon sized dollop into each cake case.

Bake in the over for 20 minutes or until golden brown on Gas Mark 6, 200 degrees C (190 degrees for fan oven). Take out and leave to cool. While they are cooling, prepare your decorations.

You can spell out your love with sweets, making heart shapes, mouth shapes or even spelling out your initials. If you're feeling lazy, buy a ready-made cake mix and follow the instructions. Or for real cheats, buy ready-made cakes and add your own decorations.

# SAUCY SPELLING

In these days of squeezy bottles, it's easy to spell out how you feel to someone. The times when you had to thump the bottom of the bottle to make the stuff come out are long gone, and now it's easy to get creative with sauces.

If you're serving up food like sausages and fries, try criss crossing the sausages to symbolise one big kiss and serve it up with a heart-shaped squirt of ketchup. If you want to say a little more, then make jumbo hot dogs and write something in mustard all the way down the length of the sausage! That way they really can eat your words.

Saying I love you with condiments is a very simple, inexpensive way to remind people just how special they are to you. You can squirt a message in mayonnaise on their open-topped sandwich, or create a ditsy little mustard heart on their burger.

For those who aren't keen on sauces, try something different. If you're serving fish, instead of garnishing it with a wedge of lemon, cut a whole slice and trim it until it's heart-shaped.

If you're preparing a salad garnish, try cutting some cucumber into hearts and criss cross slices of pepper into kisses. Not only will it be gorgeous to look at, but healthy too!

GET CREATIVE WITH SAUCES

# COOKIE LOVE

**W**e all love yummy cookies! To make a real impression, cook them yourself. Cookies are a rough and ready choice, so we've chosen some melt in the mouth Shortbread Biscuits for you to try. The benefit of this recipe is that it creates a dough that you can roll and cut into the shapes of your choice, whether it's hearts or stars, the world is your oyster!

Ingredients:

- 200 g / 7 oz / 2 cups butter, softened
- 100 g / 3.5 oz / 1 cup icing (confectioners') sugar
- 200 g / 7 oz / 2 cups plain (all-purpose) flour
- 100 g / 3.5 oz / 1 cup cornflour (cornstarch)
- Pinch of salt
- Caster sugar for decoration

Method:
First, mix the butter and icing sugar together until nice and soft. Gradually add the plain flour, cornflour and salt. Knead until smooth then roll out on a floured board. You want the dough to be about 5 mm thick.
Cut them into the shapes you desire and place on an ungreased baking tray. Bake at 180°C (160°C fan) gas 4 for about 15-25 minutes until light golden brown. Sprinkle with caster sugar while cooling and serve.

To make these extra special, decorate a box with photographs of you both together. Add some coloured tissue paper and pop a few cookies in. Then close and tie with a ribbon in their favorite color.

# EGGY HEART

Y ou've heard of the Billy Ray Cyrus hit Achy Breaky Heart. Well, forget that one, here we have an eggy bready heart! This one is great fun to do but it might need a few practice runs before you get it perfect. You will need a thick sliced piece of bread. Either use a heart-shaped cutter or a knife to carve out a heart shape in the middle of the bread, making sure you save the bread heart.

Next, heat some oil or butter in a pan. Swirl it round so that the surface is coated. Place the slice of bread in the pan (and the bread heart) and fry them lightly on one side. Flip it over and gently break an egg into the heart-shaped space. Keep an eye on it until it is nice and firm then slip it on to a plate with the fried bread heart as garnish. Delicious!

You could extend this idea by making a 'hearty' omelette. Make several heart shapes from pieces of bread, slices of cheese, or ham. Heat some oil or butter in a frying pan. While it is heating, whisk a couple of eggs. If using bread hearts, place them onto the pan first, then carefully add the whisked eggs. Let the omelette start to solidify then add the cheese and ham hearts. Keep a close eye on it so that it doesn't burn.

Next comes the tricky part, serving it up. Get a large flat plate and as carefully as you can, gradually slip the omelette on to the plate so that it stays flat and all the lovely bread, cheese and ham hearts are evident for all to see. Yum!

# PREPARE

 **love**

# PLATE

# PRESENTATION IS KEY

**V**irtually any food can become a way to say 'I Love you.' If you thought it was impossible to be romantic with carrots, then think again! It's the presentation that counts. Criss cross carrots into x shapes or shape a salad into a heart with a tomato flower in the centre.

There are plenty of things in the shops to help you make things look more than good enough to eat. You can get heart-shaped bowls, cutters and ice cube trays. You can even get a heart-shaped fondue set if you fancy getting romantic with cheese.

Cold foods in particular work really well if you're feeling amorous. They also have the advantage that you can get them ready ahead of time. If you're planning a laid-back evening then why not prepare a love plate.

Gather together lots of nibbly foods that you can share. Set mini sausages so they look like a row of kisses, pop some humous or sour cream dip in a heart-shaped bowl. For extra colour add some 'hugs' of cherry tomatoes. Get a star-shaped cookie cutter and stamp out some star-shapes from slices of cheese to show them that they are the star in your life.

For lovers with a sweet tooth, it's just as easy. Choose chocolate. Browse the aisles of the supermarket for something that little bit different. Go to a different shop from your usual place to give you inspiration. If you know they are trying to be healthy you can make sweet dips from love-colored yoghurts, strawberry or passion fruit for starters. Then slice strawberries, pineapple and kiwi, perfect for dipping and oh so virtuous too.

# APHRODISIAC TREATS

amed after Aphrodite, the Greek goddess of love, certain foods are said to have aphrodisiac qualities as they are supposed to heighten sexuality and help you feel sexy. No one really knows if there is any truth in this, or whether it's just a myth. Foods which are considered to be aphrodisiacs include:

• Almonds: try serving almond marzipan chocolates after dinner.

• Asparagus: serve steamed with butter.

• Chocolate: the Aztecs believed this was the nourishment of the Gods.

• Carrots: woo them with carrot cake.

• Honey: In medieval times men offered their partners mead, a fermented brew made from honey. The word honeymoon even comes from the fact that people drank mead as honey was supposed to make marriage sweet.

• Oysters: the Romans thought these made people seriously amorous. One to try when you're feeling rich, as they can be expensive.

• Strawberries: rich, red and lush, plus they taste brilliant, are packed with vitamin C and low in calories.

set about

SURPRISING

THEM

# COLORFUL CUISINE

**W**hat's their favourite color? Find out and then set about surprising them with a meal that reflects their top shade. For instance, if they love red, get extra romantic with a starter of stuffed tomatoes, followed by a juicy steak and finish off with a super dessert of juicy strawberries.

Always make sure the table reflects the color theme too, with napkins, flowers and decorations. You might be wondering about the more awkward colors, here are a couple more to give you inspiration:

Purple

To start: steamed purple asparagus with herb butter and crusty bread.
Main course: how about ratatouille, a well-known tasty stew featuring the lovely purple eggplant. Serve with a steak or chicken. You can simply pan fry eggplant in olive oil and garlic if that's easier.
Serve with purple sprouting broccoli.
Dessert: fresh fruit of grapes. Or maybe a delicious blackcurrant sorbet, blackberry and apple crumble or a delicious blackcurrant trifle.

Blue

To start: celery and blue Stilton soup.
Main course: try something like roast pork served with blueberry chutney. You can find this in specialist stores or find a recipe and make your own.
Dessert – blueberries and cream. Bliss!

# HAMPER DELIGHT

Grab a wicker basket and cram it with all the things they love. If you can't lay your hands on a basket, then find a box and dress it up by wrapping it in check paper like a bistro-style tablecloth. Keep an eye on the things they really love to eat and find out what's on their yummy wish list. You have several choices: do an entire 'meal in a hamper' or go for a savory or sweet option.

A savory hamper could be crammed with things like pâté, cheese and crackers. Choose some unusual stuff. For example, if they like olives don't just buy any olives but choose big fat juicy ones from Greece, or olives marinated in flavored oils. If they love Brussels pate, choose a different type, go for venison pâté or a different brand of the one they love. If they adore French cheese then buy the Camembert they love but add another option too, like Brie or Stilton.

You can have real fun with a hamper for someone with a sweet tooth. You could do a 'through the day' hamper, starting with sweet breakfast treats like croissants, through to teatime. Cram a few fresh scones in there, complete with a little pot of cream. Tuck a few chewy cookies in there too, along with some really lovely, velvety chocolates. Add some of their favourite beverages for sweet-toothed types there is lots of choice, from vanilla shakes to hot cocoa.

The wonderful thing about creating your own hamper is that you can fit it to your budget, you can spend as much or as little as you like!

all the THINGS they LOVE

broaden THEIR HORIZONS

# OVER THE TOP

This is not something you'll do very often but it really works and raises a lovely smile for the person you're treating. As you leave the house, ask your partner if they need anything. They might just want you to pick up a packet of mints for them. Instead of picking one, pick five or six different types and go completely over the top.

This also works if they ask you to buy them a bar of chocolate. Surprise them with many different bars, especially ones you think they'll love but probably haven't tried yet.

When you get back and they ask you if you've remembered the item, get your secret store out, one at a time, and watch their reaction as they realise how thoughtful you are!

This is a really fun idea and can help broaden their horizons too. Always get the exact thing they've asked for and then use your imagination to choose extras. For example if they always drink a Kenyan blend of coffee, buy that but also choose a Colombian blend and a Mocha blend for them to try.

You never know, one of those might become a new favorite! The same applies for cookies. If they always opt for chocolate ones then by all means buy those, but also buy them a few different ones to try, after all, variety is the spice of life!

How often have you heard others criticise their partners for having a lack of imagination? Well, with this thoughtful act feel free to be as imaginative as you like!

# CARE AND SHARE

Some foods were just made for sharing and they are a wonderful way of sharing time with someone special. All kinds of hot and cold food lend themselves to this kind of extra special togetherness.

Many of the best sharing foods are finger foods, inevitably. Think of the most obvious and move on from there. Order a great big pizza and when you cut the slices they are so big it takes two to handle them! Or order two smaller pizzas and swap, feeding each other makes eating pepperoni more passion-filled!

Go American style, lots of US foods lend themselves to a joint experience. Try making your own southern fried chicken together. Follow the recipe and have a cuddle while it sizzles in the pan. Eating the food you've just cooked will give you a nice warm feeling.

Chips and dips are great to share too. Slice up stacks of cucumber and peppers, add a few tortilla chips and some breadsticks and get dipping. Make sure you have more than one dip to choose from, such as taramasalata, sour cream and chives or humous.

If you like a bit of a kick to your dips, go for hot salsa and guacamole. You could even sprinkle some cheese on the chips and warm them in the oven for a few minutes for a mexican-style finish!

# MADE

## for

## sharing

# CREATE a

# CINEMA

# experience

# POPCORN CLASSICS

What better way to spend some quality time with your partner than to cosy up together and have movie night. Going to the cinema can be very expensive. The price of the tickets is manageable but it's all the refreshments that end up breaking the bank and ends up turning it into a very expensive date.

So, why not try to create a cinema experience at home? By watching two movies in the space of a night it makes for fair play. You can choose one you like and they can choose one they like. Try to pick different types of movies; don't go for two action thrillers or two animations in one sitting. Mix and match works best.

Before you settle down for the evening, prepare everything you need. Popcorn is an essential! Buy your own popping corn and do it yourself, or cheat and choose the microwavable stuff. Many supermarkets also sell it ready popped, sweet, salty, toffee-coated or buttery, buy all four if you can't decide!

Get everything ready in the kitchen before the opening scenes. If you're popping your own corn then do that first. Try getting exotic with it, many specialist shops sell different flavors of corn to pop at home. Buy a few different types of sweets and chocolates so you can both create your own delicious mix. For a real cinema experience, buy some disposable cups and bowls.

Next, you need to plan your timing. Check the running times of the film. Plan to have popcorn during the first film, a break in the middle if you need a hot dog (unless you're too full!) and then make the second film your sweets feature.

# MAKE SWEET MEMORIES

Talking about your childhood can be huge fun. Try taking it one step further and see if you can find out all their old favorites. Remember going to the sweet shop with coins clutched in your hand? Think back to the trouble you had deciding whether or not to have some sweets weighed out or to pick lots of single sweets instead.

Well, recreate that experience by searching for the sweets and treats of yesteryear. Chances are you can still get all the things that they adored when they were children. Make sure you buy enough of all the sweets so you can share.

One great way to get to know people better is to find out what they like and why. Next, make a date. Even if you've been married for years, arrange to meet them at the local playground. Try and pick a time when it's quieter so you can sit side by side on the swings together.

When you get there, remind them that they once told you about their favourite sweets. Then either pluck a sweet out of your pocket or produce a bag crammed with them. Try and make sure it's a paper bag for those excited moments of rustling, they'll be delighted.

Work your way through the bag together, sampling all the delights and reminisce your favorite childhood memories!

# CHERISHED

## times

# THE FIRST TIME

D o you remember the first thing you ate together? Whether you have been together for 5 months or 50 years, you can still probably remember what you ate and where it was. Whether it was a hot dog at the fairground or a gourmet meal in a posh restaurant, then do it again.

Your partner will be amazed that you can remember the first thing you shared together. It could be a trigger for a great few days of cherished times together. Maybe you differ in you memories of exactly what food you first shared? If this is the case then re-visit both versions for added fun.

To make this more memorable, try and arrange to recreate your first meal in situ. So if you were sheltering under an umbrella in the rain when you should have been picnicking, then get out there and do it again!

If you were on a train when the carriages were stuck in a tunnel and you shared a dried up sandwich and a melted chocolate bar then take a rail trip somewhere. Although the train might not stop in a tunnel, you get the idea!

If it was a restaurant, then that's easier, but make sure you call ahead and see if you can arrange to have the same table you originally sat on. Check out the menu to see if the choices you made the first time round are still on the menu.

If the restaurant is no longer in business, then go somewhere else to have the meal, or if you're feeling creative, cook it at home, recreating the ambience using candles and your best table linen.

# Ways to Say I Love You...

## MAKE

# JAR OF MEMORIES

This is a fabulous way of reminding them what makes your relationship so special. Buy one of those big glass storage jars available in kitchen shops. Then choose a pad of paper in different shades of their favourite colour.

Every time you think of something good you have done together, jot it down and put it into the jar. When it's full, wrap it up and leave it where they can find it.

If you're not sure what memories to include, rest assured they can be absolutely anything! They can be as mundane or as saucy as you like. For instance, you might remember the time you got caught in the rain and got soaked through. Remind them how it felt when you were warming each other up!

It doesn't matter if you've been together for months or years, there will be plenty of things that your partner will be thrilled to remember. If you need some inspiration to get you going, try looking back through old photographs, this will surely spark lots of memories.

You could even add the photographs to the jar to help bring the memories alive. If you are unable to acquire a storage jar, then a box will work just as well. Tie it with beautiful ribbon for extra effect and then hand your loved one their very own treasure trove of memories.

thrilled to remember

UP close and PERSONAL

# CREATIVE CREATION

Yes, you can easily buy a card, but homemade is so much better and the craft shops these days offer beautiful finishing touches to make your card perfect. Take a few minutes to browse the aisles. You can get cards in all colours and buy a fantastical array of things to decorate them with. Card making is all about getting up close and personal.

Think about the things they like. Maybe he's really into old cars or his passion is golf. Maybe she has a shoe fetish or goes wild for jazzy handbags. Whatever it is, you will be able to find something connected to their passions.

Plan ahead. What is the card for? A birthday, an anniversary or just because? Make sure you keep it secret, as a surprise isn't a surprise anymore if it means that they've seen a whole load of new craft items lying around the house.

Give yourself plenty of time to plan a design. Scribble down your ideas on scrap paper and experiment with upright cards and cards in different shapes. A lot of the decorations available are already sticky, which saves time and mess with glue.

Pop on some of their favourite music to get you in the mood for creativity. Add letters or ribbons and if you're feeling really arty, you can even make a pop-up card.

Now comes the best bit, what to write inside.? You can keep it cryptic, be short and sweet or wax lyrical about what makes them wonderful to you. Just enjoy yourself! You never know, one little card may turn into a whole new hobby.

# DELIGHTFUL GEMS

e're not suggesting you become a goldsmith, just develop a few fun ways to make them smile by coming up with a spot of home-made jewellery. Making them a personalised necklace or bracelet using beads is one of the easiest things to do. It doesn't require any specialist skills – and it's a cheap one to do!

Trawl the craft stores and markets for beads and string then off you go. Choose beads in their favourite colour and buy a few alphabet beads so you can say what you like. You could just add their name or include a little message.

Make a love bracelet – or make two of them, one for them and one for you. For real cuteness, make them both identical and promise that neither of you will take them off. You can adapt friendship bracelet kits to make these or just buy several colours of embroidery cotton and weave or plait them. Make a little ceremony of it by presenting them with their love bracelet and asking them to help tie yours too.

These days jewellery can be made from virtually anything. You probably remember making pasta jewellery at school. We're not suggesting you go quite that retro but you'd be surprised at quite what you can use – wooden beads, strips of leather, all sorts. And for real fun, what about food jewellery?

Make a 'jewel' necklace from little jellies. Thread a needle with thick embroidery cotton and skewer a row of jellies into a necklace. Then give it to your partner and nibble away at the sweets on their neck. It could lead to a real gem of an evening…

85

TRAWl

the

STORES

CARRY THOUGHTS of

YOU around

# SPECIAL TOKEN

This little memento is a great way for your loved one to carry thoughts of you round, everywhere they go. Basic key rings are easy to find in all kinds of shops, but craft shops also sell clear snap-open key rings so you can add your own picture.

It doesn't have to be quite that simple though. Why not personalise it more and make things more cryptic. Here are just a few ideas:

- Add a leaf of their favorite tree.
- Press a petal from their favorite flower.
- Draw a self-portrait and sign it.
- Include a lock of hair from your head
- If you've been together for many years, enclose an old photograph, dating from the early days of your courtship.
- Include a picture of the very first house you lived in.

There are plenty of other ways to personalise a key ring that can just be added to the existing 'ring.' How about plaiting some wool in shades of their favourite colour to create a 'friendship key ring' or write a little poem and get it laminated so that they can read it whenever they feel like it.

Finally presentation is key. Wrap the key ring up in some tissue paper and leave it somewhere they wouldn't expect to find it. Or, you could surprise them by placing it on their bunch of keys when they're not looking.

# PICTURE PERFECT

They are everywhere, aren't they? Ask most people the one thing they would try and save (apart from their family) in the event of a fire and the vast majority would say their photographs. We've all got shots of friends and family dotted around the house, and chances are, most of us have bundles in drawers and cupboards.

A great gift is to compile your own album specially for them. It can be anything you like. You can spend time putting all the family photographs into their neat little slots, or you can choose to theme the album, for instance, holidays.

Creating an album is a wonderful gift after a big event, not just for weddings. If you've taken lots of shots on your seaside holiday then take time to put them all into a special book. Personalise it with a trip to a craft store where you can buy stickers with a seaside theme.

Although it's easy to buy a photo album, you can make your own if you are feeling creative. Use a scrapbook to include all those precious memories and get ready to tell a story in pictures

If you do this, you could also add other mementos that go with the photographs. For example, if you are putting together a holiday album, add tickets for things like train rides, concerts and sports events. You could even add a menu from your favorite eatery.

# compile your own ALBUM

like

TELLING

A

STORY

# INTIMATE SCRAPBOOK

This is a great one for special events. It doesn't have to be about a birthday or a party, it could be things like the weeks when you were getting your first child ready to go to school, or the time when you decided to give the garden a makeover.

Making a scrapbook is like telling a story, only it's the best story because it's all about you and your life together. For example, if you decide to revamp the garden, then make sure you take lots of before and after photographs to include and make a note of all the things you found when you were clearing the ground.

Give each page a heading and a timeline to show progress. It's all too easy to confine our memories to the monumental events, like getting married and having a baby. But so many of life's experiences would benefit from being recorded in this way.

Why don't you try making a scrapbook about your first year together, or the first time you moved in together? Include photographs and little stories depicting the events.

If you have a pet, think about the time you brought it home. Remember how tiny they were or how they liked to sleep your arms. Include things they have outgrown, such as collars and toys.

Scrapbooking also makes a great gift for relatives who can't be around too much. Nowadays social networking forms a big part of communication, but sometimes it's also lovely to have something physical to hold in your hands to remind you of the highs of living.

## PERSONAL COLLECTION

veryone loves a good song, and chances are, your loved one has an absolute stack of them. But even in the days of MP3 players and iPods, do they really have all their favorites to hand, when they want them. This is a task for the super-orderly. Stop and consider just how they would best like their songs to be organised and then create a series of CDs for them or buy them an MP3 and load songs in a certain order.

There are loads of ways to do this. For instance, you could put together a load of tracks from each decade. Or you could divide their music loves into genres: soul, rock, pop and classical. How about making a music soundtrack of your life together, from the first song you ever danced together to, or the music you had at your wedding.

Compiling a collection of their favorite songs is quite simple to do and makes a terrific gift. If you pop them on to a CD, then slip it into their car so that when they turn on the ignition in the morning, their favorites will start blasting out. Stick a post-it sticker on the steering wheel to let them know what you've done.

If you have plenty of time, you can make a whole series of CDs chronicling their changing musical tastes throughout the years. Decorate the covers by including a few key dates: the first time you met, the first time you said I Love You, the day you got engaged or your first holiday together.

create

A WHOLE

SERIES

DISAPPEAR

behind **THE**

COVERS

# READING PLEASURE

If the one you love has a hectic and busy life but loves nothing better than to disappear behind the covers of a great book, then this one is a sure-fire winner. Sometimes it seems impossible to find the time to sit down in perfect peace and immerse yourself in a good novel.

As a treat to your loved one, why not make it possible. First of all, check out the sort of books they like. Do they have a favorite author: Jackie Collins, Val McDermid, Stephen King, or do they prefer to read books in a specific genre, sci-fi, crime or romance?

Once you have done your homework, head to a good bookshop and choose a book for them. That's half the job. Next, set about making them a bookmark. It's a perfect way of surprising a keen reader with a little love note. Make the bookmark long enough to stick out of the top of the book, so they don't lose their place.

Then, write your own note on the bookmark and slot it inside. Make sure they have time to sit and read. If you have children, then plan to take them out for a few hours. If it's just the two of you, make yourself scarce.

If they have a crazy life where every minute seems to be filled up, then reading can sometimes seem like a guilty pleasure! If you're really not sure what book to buy them, make the bookmark and drive them to a bookstore. Tell them you'll wait while they choose and once home, leave them to immerse themselves in their very own private reading world.

# EXCLUSIVE COUPONS

If you want to do them a favor or a fair few favors, then create a booklet of coupons especially for them, with their own dedicated offers and treats. Make the booklet as simple or as elaborate as you fancy, just a few pieces of paper stapled together detailing your acts of goodwill will suffice.

So, what sort of things should you include? This is where it gets very personal. What would please one person could annoy another so make sure you really know what they would appreciate. The idea is that they can redeem their coupons at any time.

Your coupons could include:

- Wash and clean their car, inside and out.
- Washing the dishes for a week.
- A meal out at a restaurant of their choice.
- Their choice of TV programme for one night.
- An offer to run them a bath.
- Breakfast in bed.
- Doing the supermarket shopping.
- A back rub after a long day.
- A foot massage
- A lift to and from a night out.

CREATE

DIFFERENT

ATMOSPHERES

# INTIMATE ATMOSPHERE

If we all conducted our lives in a blaze of bright lights, we would probably never get romantic at all. Different types of lighting can create different atmospheres, so experiment and try a few of these simple techniques.

Candles. Obviously you have to be extra vigilant with these because of the fire hazard, but candles can create all types of mood. If your other half comes home tired, what better way to say I Love You than running them a deep bubbly bath and lighting a few scented tea lights for added chill-factor.

On a late summer evening, create a sense of romance with outdoor lighters. Again, you can use candles here. Choose nice terracotta pots to put them in and to prevent them from blowing out.

When indoors why don't you opt for a light tree? Garden centres sell lovely dried branches for indoor use. Pop them in an empty vase and then string fairy lights round them.

Lamps. Switch off the overhead lights and opt for low-down lamp lighting. Everything looks better in subdued lighting and keeping the lights low instantly gives the room a huge sense of relaxation. You can just relax and enjoy each other's company or use it to get romantic!

Take a torch. A night walk with the one you love can be wonderfully adorable. People talk differently to each other as they stroll along, hand in hand, gazing up at the starry sky. ! If it's a cloudy night, flick on your torch and cuddle up close to each other as you make your way home.

# CARTOON LOVE

an't draw? Who cares? Get out your pens and pencils and get sketching. One of the best things to do is try and pen a cartoon of your loved one, or even a caricature. If you have ever seen caricature artists at work, you'll realise that they pick out certain features and emphasise them. So this one calls for subtlety and sensitivity.

Instead, concentrate on the things you like about them. Think back to what attracted you to your loved one. Does he have gorgeous blue eyes? Are her cheekbones to die for? What about that cute little dimple in her right cheek, or the funny way his hair curls? Get some artists' pencils, a 2B and a 4B for shading and have a go.

If you have some spare cash, then you could get someone to draw the caricature for you. Get together a handful of photographs that show your loved one in the best light. Make sure you brief the artist on what you want, something flattering and gorgeous. Then get it framed and present it to them so you can both have a really good giggle!

If you think a caricature is too hard for you to do, try a cartoon strip starring your partner. Make it funny and silly. If you really can't draw, use stick people but give them your lover's name and traits. The key is to get personal on paper and give your loved one something to cherish forever.

# Cartoon

## Of your

LOVED one

# FLOWER POWER

**Y**ou don't have to go to town on beautiful bouquets of shop-bought flowers. There are plenty of ways to say I Love You with flowers of a different kind. Start by making them their very own daisy chain.

Choose a lovely sunny day, pack a picnic and get making. Pick a pile of white-petal daisies, make a little slit in the base of each stem and thread them all together.

Pick a few gorgeous yellow meadow buttercups, tell them to tip up their chin and if there is a yellow reflection, old wives' tales say it means you like butter. Of course, it seems that everyone likes butter!

Pick pussy willows. A great rite of spring, the sight of these fluffy little catkins brings joy to the hearts of anyone keen to see the back of winter chills. Pick a few twigs and pop them in a vase to bring a spot of spring to the one you love.

Blossom. A definite sign that summer is round the corner is trees draped in frilly pink and white blooms. Pick a couple of branches and bring blossom indoors. Among the prettiest are apple and cherry blossom.

Go rural. Not exactly flowers, but select a few hedgerow grasses and bring the country into the kitchen. Steer clear of wild flowers, as many are protected and it's illegal to uproot a wild flower without the permission of the landowner.

# SWEETIE PIE

We can all go to the shops and buy a bag of sweets, now try and make some. You can do this as a surprise or put on a pair of matching aprons and try it together. There's nothing quite like mixing your own delicious treats and then sampling them together later.

There are some very complicated sweet recipes out there, but this one is super-simple and makes a great gift for special occasions too. You can double this recipe if you want to make lots.

Coconut Ice Drops

- 200 g / 7 oz / 2 cups condensed milk
- 230 g / 8 oz / 1 cup icing (confectioners') sugar
- 170 g / 6 oz / 3/4 cup desiccated coconut
- Red food colouring

Mix the icing sugar and coconut together and stir in the condensed milk. Knead into a firm dough. Split the dough in half and colour one half with a drop of red food colouring to create a romantic pink shade. Roll both pieces to the same shape and put them together. Leave them to chill and then cut into squares.

# MIXING your OWN delicious TREATS

# SHAKE IT UP

It's true that you can uncork a bottle of wine or crack open a can of beer, but just for a change make cocktails together. It's fun, creative and a great way to try new drinks. They don't even need to contain alcohol. Work out what you need to create the cocktails and go shopping first.

There's nothing worse than getting ready to create your liquid masterpiece and then find out that you're missing a key ingredient! Get yourself a cocktail shaker, a couple of glasses and try these out.

Cosmopolitan: a pink drink that tastes as good as it looks.
You will need:

- 40 ml Vodka
- 15 ml triple sec
- 20 ml cranberry juice
- 10 ml freshly squeezed lime juice

Put some ice in the shaker, add all the ingredients. Shake vigorously then pour into a martini glass.

Cinderella: a non-alcoholic mix that shows you too can go to the ball!
You will need:

- Equal parts of pineapple, orange and lemon juice
- Soda water
- Grenadine
- Fruit to decorate

Mix the fruit juices together and pour over ice cubes into a tall glass. Top up with soda water and add a generous dash of grenadine.

# READY TEDDY

Everyone loves a teddy bear. Small and cute, giant and fluffy, these cuddly toys come in all shapes and sizes. Now it's time to use them to get love on your side. A teddy bear always brings a smile to people's faces. The shops are filled with thousands of them, from solidly stuffed old-fashioned bears to floppy ones with silly grins.

You could just go out and buy a bear to say I Love You or you could make one, but for most us this will be too hard. One way to make the gift of a teddy bear more intimate and special is to ensure the bear gives the message you want to get across, your adoration.

Let the teddy do the talking! You could write a little message to your loved one and tie it to its paw, slip a truffle selection on to its lap, pop some jewellery you've bought them into a little box and tape it to the teddy bear's paws or sit it in the front seat of their car with a list of directions to their favourite restaurant.

Of course it doesn't have to be a teddy bear, a soft toy of your choice would work just as well, especially if it is an animal they adore. Anything soft and cuddly is a sure-fire way to cheer up even the most down hearted soul. So, when you think they need a fillip, get creative and make your teddy the bearer of loving words, little treats and use it as a messenger. Think of soft toys as a cuddly version of Cupid and his bow and arrow!

all

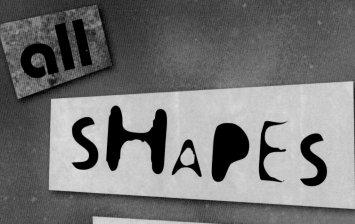

SHAPES

AND

sizes

MAKE A MODEL OF YOUR LOVE

# MODEL CREATION

We're not expecting you to strike a pose on the catwalk or hit the big fashion shows in Paris or New York. This one's more of a creative idea using modelling clay to make a model of your love!

You could do this one together. Making models isn't just for children, you know. It's a cheap and cheerful way to spend an afternoon and the models you create out of the soft, pliable stuff can be as silly or as saucy as you like.

If you fancy making a model as a surprise then use it as a hint of things to come. For example, if you're heading off for a Mediterranean beach holiday soon, grab some yellow dough and create a sun with a big fat smile on its face. If you're planning to chill out with some fast food and a movie, make a pretend plate of burger and chips, just like you did when you were kids.

You can spell out your love too. Some types of modelling clay turn hard if you leave it out, so work quickly and keep it short and sweet. If you're modelling to make love tokens then make sure you leave them where they can't be discovered while they dry out.

But the most fun you'll have is playing at being young again. Whether you're 20 or 80, sit down together at the kitchen table and get modelling. Make snakes and cakes and spotty dogs. Compete with each other to see who can make the wackiest creature around. Decide before you start what the prize is and remember, you're grown-ups, it can be as naughty as you like!

# HANGING GIFTS

**M**ake it completely clear how you feel about them by creating a window hanging that announces it! You can choose a number of ways to do this. Get some clear peel-off paper. Cut out felt shapes including hearts, words, whatever you like. Stick them on to the paper and then stick the paper on to the window.

Make them a stained 'glass' heart, using see-through paper in different colours such as red, yellow and greens. When you hang them up in the light your love will shine through. Get your message across before they even step through the door, by creating a love token that you can attach to the door knocker. This can be as serious or as silly as you like.

For example, try making a stuffed heart. Take two pieces of felt in their favourite colour and cut out a heart shape. Either glue round the edges or stitch, leaving a small opening. Put cotton wool or other stuffing inside it, then glue or stitch up the closure. Glue or sew a loop of ribbon to the top of the heart and hook on to the door to give them a really warm loving welcome.

If you know when they are due to arrive back make them some heart-shaped cookies. Use any simple recipe, roll out the dough and cut it into heart shapes, adding a hole in the middle. This is where the ribbon will go. When they are cooked and cooled, thread ribbon through the hole and tie them to the door handle for a tasty welcome.

get YOUR

message

across

# Ways to Say I Love You...

# GETAWAYS

MAKE a real day OF it

# ANIMAL LOVE

**W**hen was the last time you went to the zoo? Chances are it was long ago and you probably haven't been as a couple. It's somewhere we all go as children with our parents or on a school trip, but as adults it simply slips our mind.

One of the loveliest things about a trip to the zoo is that it teaches you so much more about your loved one. You get to know all about their favorite animals. Wherever you live, you're not far from a zoo or wildlife park. If you can, choose a day during the week when it's likely to be quieter.

Then off you go! Zoos are big places so get a guide and work out what you want to see first. If watching the penguins being fed is a priority, find out when that happens and work everything else around it. Don't forget the reptile house either. That's a great opportunity to get snuggled up as you go round and look at the giant tarantulas and scaly lizards.

As you wander round, you'll find many 'human' traits in some of the animals you're looking at. The wonderful way the mum elephant snuggles up to her baby, or the way the chimpanzees loll around on the swings! Many zoos nowadays have massive conservation programmes, so you'll get to see what they are doing to protect endangered species and encourage breeding programmes for them.

If the zoo you choose to visit is a long distance away, make a real day of it. Pack a picnic or plan to eat in one of their cafes or restaurants. Remember to leave room for a tasty ice cream or yummy lollipop. Spend some time wandering around the gift shop, you could buy each other a cuddly animal toy to remind you of your day out.

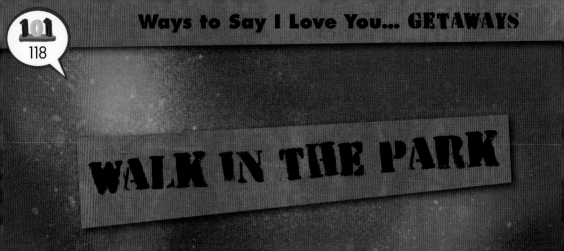

# WALK IN THE PARK

You drive past it every day but when was the last time you stopped for a walk in the park? Now's the time to familiarise yourself with your local neighborhood. Every town has a park or open space so take the time to enjoy it with the one you love.

Pick a day when it looks like it's going to be nice weather. Pack a little picnic or a bunch of snacks. Depending on the time of year, take a flask of soup or cocoa or cool some drinks before you go. Then get walking! When you're on foot you spot things you never see from the car, and it gives you a chance to talk in a different way. It's a terrific way of stepping off the treadmill of your busy life for a few hours and really taking time to reacquaint yourself with the person you love.

Depending on the type of park you go to there will be all kinds of opportunities to take the air and generally relax. Wander close to the water and feed the ducks, take five minutes to sit on the swings and reminisce about your favorite childhood playground times. Have a go on the swings or climbing frame!

If it's spring, pick a few blossoms in bloom and take them home. In autumn see if you can find any horse chestnut trees and search for conkers. Run through the leaves, kicking them in the air. You could even collect a few and create a collage memory of your day out together when you get back.

take the time to ENJOY it

# FIRST MEETING

Everyone remembers their first meeting so why not go back to the place you first met? If it's far away, even in another country, make the effort and go there. If possible try and revisit the place of your first meeting at the same time of year, for example, if you met in February on the top deck of a number 28 bus then do it again.

If your eyes met theirs over a piña colada on a Jamaican beach then get saving and get over there. The place you first met is very different from your actual first date. Unless you had a blind date, it's most likely that the formal bit came later.

Maybe you met when your puppy ran across the park crashing into their Labrador? Or perhaps you collided in the pasta aisle of the supermarket while searching for red pesto? Everyone's first meeting is unique and this is a fun way to revisit the past.

Perhaps the man of your dreams swept into your life with a ladder when he turned up to clean the windows? Maybe the girl you know love was nothing more than  a voice on the end of the phone for a long time? Maybe they were the person with the big head who blocked the screen in front of you at the cinema!!

Plan to go back to the site of your first meeting together. If you like, you can even re-enact the scenario. But one of the best approaches is to go back to the place and then go for a meal to celebrate how far you've come.

A lot of first introductions are simply by chance. You could both spend some time imagining what life would have been like if you hadn't met, and then fallen for, the partner of your dreams!

# THEME PARK MAGIC

This is one of the best ways to really get to know each other, even if you thought you had a very good idea of their likes and dislikes. Theme parks are a scream- literally! If you're not much of an adrenaline junkie, there's sure to be something you can go on, even if it's a nice sedate ride like the teacups.

All over the world, there are plenty of theme parks to choose from, so there's bound to be one near you! You can incorporate the overseas ones into the holiday of a lifetime or stay closer to home and just go for the day.

A visit is a great way to forget all your cares and just be a kid again. They are places where it's perfectly acceptable to queue for the scariest riders, terrify yourself witless and then queue up and do it all over again. At parks with the most in-demand rides, it's a good idea to get there early. If they're a long distance away, it might be worth going up the night before and staying at a budget hotel not far from the park entrance.

Try and give yourself plenty of variety, from the heart-stopping, big drop rides, to the old school fun ones like the carousel and the bumper cars. Theme parks offer you plenty of opportunity to shop, too. A visit isn't complete without buying souvenirs in the gift shop and going home with a bag stacked with cute mementos to cherish.

FORGET all your CARES

# REAL TEST of your LOVE

# SWEET COMPROMISE

This is a real test of your love – to spend time with them doing something they love, even though you loathe it. If ballet is their thing and you can't stand the sight of people prancing around, then bite the bullet and book a couple of tickets to a ballet show. Ask them for background on the story you're going to see and see if you can find a way to rise above your dislike and allow yourself to enjoy it!

If they are a crazy mad football fan and you can't stand the sight of the pitch let alone the players, then swallow your pride and get on the terraces. Make a point of learning the names of the players and read up on the latest results so that when you get there you're not clueless.

Maybe they love curry but your idea of a good meal is something plain like steak and chips. Book a nice table at an Indian restaurant and give it a try. There's nothing more heartwarming than a partner making the effort to try something new. Ask their advice on what to order and tuck in, you might surprise yourself!

The same goes for hobbies. Maybe they love fishing or dancing but the thought leaves you cold. Ask if you can go with them once in a while and be prepared to enjoy yourself. If it's something like dancing or ice skating, don't worry if you can't remember the moves or slither all over the rink, just have a laugh. It will bring you closer in the end.

The big advantage of doing something you don't like is that if really, in your absolute heart of hearts, you don't like it, at least you can say you gave it a shot. You'll both have a lot more respect for each other as a result!

# KARAOKE LOVE

If you sing like Lady Gaga or Elvis or if your version of crooning is totally off key, don't let that worry you, just let rip and sing anyway. Next time you're in a bar together and there's a karaoke evening, don't just talk about getting up there on the microphone, actually get up and do it.

It doesn't matter if you crunch through the keys or fluff the lyrics, they'll love you for it. A couple of drinks first might be what you need for a spot of Dutch courage and take the edge off your nerves. But what should you sing?

Choose something you love or that you know will make them laugh. You could even persuade them to do a duet with you! Remember, listen carefully for your cue, follow the words on the screen and don't forget to breathe! Here are some song ideas:

For Him

- Boys II Men – I'll Make Love to You
- Marvin Gaye – Let's Get it On
- Queen – You're My Best Friend
- Elton John – Your Song
- The Beatles – Love Me Do

For Her:

- Whitney Houston – I Will Always Love You
- Norah Jones – Don't Know Why
- Alicia Keys – If I Ain't got You
- Eva Cassidy – Songbird
- Tina Turner – Simply The Best

# ANNIVERSARY TREAT

No matter what day your anniversary falls, always make a point of ensuring you're not at work that day. When we say anniversary, it can be anything you like, the anniversary of the day you met, the day you married or the day you first moved in together. It doesn't matter, so long as it's special to you.

With our hectic lives, it's easy to let special days fall by the wayside but make sure you don't let that happen. This can be a day when you both go incognito: no emails, no phone calls and if you stay at home, don't answer the door.

Do something completely different from the norm. Maybe pick a place to go that begins with the letter of their name. You could head to the seaside, a castle or even a restaurant. The key is to make it memorable, for both of you.

If you really can't decide where to go, come up with five ideas each and put them all in a hat then pull one out. That adds to the excitement. If you're short of cash, have an 'at-home' day out, just eating together and generally relaxing.

You could go one step further and surprise your loved one. Ask them to book the day off work and tell them to be ready for a surprise. Leave little clues lying around the house relating to the place you're going.

Give them a preparation list so that they know what to wear and what to pack for the day and play some guessing games in the car to make it more fun. Your loved one is bound to be intrigued and will love and appreciate the effort and thought you put in.

# FUNFAIR DELIGHT

**Y**ou see the trucks and low loaders arrive and you know it's arrived. The sight of the funfair arriving sends a thrill through most of us and takes us back to our teenage years when we spent too long on the rides or scoffed too many hot dogs.

Whether you're a man or a woman, invite your other half to a date at the funfair and don't leave until you've won them a prize. Go on, hook a duck and win them some plastic jewellery, knock the coconuts off and go home with the hairy fruit and hack it open to drink the milk!

The funfair is all about sights and smells. Go at night when the sky is dark and the multi-colored lights beckon you in. This is the best time to go on the rides. As you spin into the air you get a twirling, whirling view of the town from the excitement of your seat.

Don't forget the ghost train. It's never really that scary but it's a great way to cuddle up together in the carriage as you trundle through a route of ghouls. When you're done, pop into the arcades and try your luck on the many gaming machines.

For added fun, invite some friends along. That way, if one of you doesn't like going on a certain ride you won't have to miss out, and whoever doesn't go on the ride can watch from the ground, snapping some memorable pictures.

# WEEKEND PAMPER

The spa experience isn't just for the ladies. Whisk yourselves away to a spa and come back pretty pampered and ridiculously relaxed. Take a weekend out for pure indulgence and you'll find that not only do you feel refreshed, but you look pretty good too.

There are health and beauty spas all over, so choose one to suit your budget. Most include three vitamin packed meals a day and some include treatments or you can tailor-make the break to suit exactly what you want.

Exercise classes and gym facilities are usually included and there is often a swimming pool, whirlpool spa and sauna on site so that you can take your time to soak and swim whenever it suits.

Imagine arriving and kicking off those restricting work clothes, slipping into a soft and fluffy bathrobe and heading for a treatment room. Among the must-dos are a facial. Let a skilled beauty therapist cleanse, exfoliate and pamper your skin. You can choose from back or full body massages, complement them with a pedicure and a manicure.

If you want to try something a little different, consider a hot stones treatment or book yourself in for some crystal therapy. These treatments can often be booked as a twosome so you can enjoy them together.

Take a couple of books you've been meaning to get round to reading, or spend your evenings just sitting and chatting. One thing's for certain, after all that indulgence, you'll both sleep well at night.

## TANDEM THRILLS

Cycling together can be great fun, but try taking it one step further and hire yourself a bicycle made for two. Plan a weekend break and hop on to the two-seater, it's a great way to get to know each other better, and it involves lots of trust too, just like the name suggests- you must do it in tandem!

Take it in turns to be the one up front (that's the job with all the work!) and really push yourself up the hills. It may sound like punishment but choose an area with plenty of ups and downs as there's nothing quite like the joy of freewheeling with the wind in your hair after all the hard work of the up-hill slog.

There are many specialised places  around offer tandems for hire and they will give you plenty of advice before you set off. Though a weekend away on a tandem is great fun, if you're trying to keep the budget low or simply haven't got the time, plenty of cities have cycle hire schemes were you can rent a tandem for half a day or a whole day.

If you decide to go for the weekend option, bear in mind that cycling is thirsty work so make sure you always have drinks on board. Book yourself into a cute hotel or head for the hills and hire a cottage for a weekend. Imagine how lovely it will be to get off your bike after a long day in the saddle and slip into a beautifully scented bath to ease those aches and pains.

seduced

# NEW YORK LOVE AFFAIR

New York, New York, so good they named it twice. Nobody can fail to be seduced by the bright lights and the friendly people in the Big Apple so head out there for a real I Love You holiday.

The place is buzzing 24 hours a day so you'll need to plan your trip carefully, otherwise you'll find yourself overwhelmed. Pick a few key things to do: visit the Statue of Liberty, go down Fifth Avenue and browse the shops, hop on the subway and treat yourselves to a delicious sandwich in one of the many delis.

Before you go, decide what you want to see. Often, trying to fit in too many things can just leave you both feeling exhausted and that will spoil things. Before you set off, make sure you've got some really comfortable shoes. New York is a city to be seen on foot and over the course of a weekend you'll find yourself walking miles.

Make sure you experience the place at all times of day. Get yourself a coffee in a café first thing and watch as the office workers head to their desks for the day. See the city from above by heading up to the Empire State Building. Hail one of the New York's famous yellow cabs to get a hands-on idea of what it's like to work your way through the traffic.

Don't forget to go to Broadway and soak up one of the many hit shows. Of course, you don't need to spend too much to enjoy the Big Apple. Just get yourself over there and take a big bite of New York life. You'll never forget it!

# ENCHANTING SEA

o matter where you live, you can manage a trip to the seaside for a day, even if it means an early start. Forget that you're grown-ups for a while and treat your trip to the coast as if you were a couple of big kids.

Start early and arrive just as the tide's going out. Pick a lovely stretch of sandy beach and then pop to one of the seafront shops for all your essentials, including buckets, spades and little paper flags to crown your creations.

Spend a morning on the beach building a castle. Don't forget to make a moat so that when the tide comes in the water will swirl round your fortress. Then take a well-earned break for lunch. Treat yourself to a delicious ice cream to round off your lunch nicely.

Don't forget your souvenirs. You'll need some sweets, sticky fudge and a few creations from the local shell shop. Then it's time to get competitive. Head for the crazy golf and don't take any prisoners. Plan to reward the one who gets a hole in one with an extra special treat – you decide what that might be!

If the place you're in has a pier then get right on it. Walk all the way down to the end and if it's sunny hire yourselves a deckchair to take in the sea air. As the bright lights of the seaside illuminations flick on, it's time to head home. You'll certainly sleep well after all that!

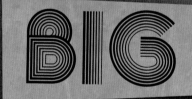

# PARISIAN PASSION

One of the most romantic places in the world, the French capital has long been a destination for lovers. And no matter how many times you visit, you'll find something new to fall in love with. You can get there pretty quickly these days, by plane, ferry or on the train with Eurostar.

Opinions vary regarding the best time of year to visit. Some say spring is perfect, when the city's many trees are in blossom, while others recommend high summer or autumn when the place is quieter. It's all down to your preference at the end of the day.

Paris is a chameleon of a destination. In other words, it can be anything you want it to be. You can treat it like a museum and visit the many treasures tucked away in the Louvre. Or, you can marvel at the wonders of its many gothic churches; the icing on the cake being the impressive Notre Dame Cathedral sitting on its own little island in the middle of the River Seine.

Above all, Paris is a city to stroll round. It's a place for people-watching and taking your time watching the world go by. Pull up at one of the many pavement cafes and take a seat. Sip a coffee or a glass of rich red wine and relax. Head up to the area of Montmartre where street artists ply their trade or visit the colourful Pigalle area with its bohemian atmosphere.

Paris can suit all budgets. Once you have arrived and have a place to stay, it's possible to enjoy the city without spending very much at all. Or if you're feeling flush you can splash out with fancy meals and even fancier shopping in the many seductive stores that line the city's streets.

# MESMERIZING EXPRESS

ook a seat on the world famous train and sit back as you travel through the glories of Europe's countryside. Made famous by Agatha Christie's Murder on the Orient Express, this grand old train sums up everything about luxury travel of yesteryear. These days, there is a choice of locations. You can still travel to Paris and Istanbul, but the service has opened up to include Venice and other European cities.

Sit back and revel in the romance of a golden age. You'll travel in original 1920s carriages with Lalique glass panels, wood burning stoves and intricate art deco relief. You can rest in vintage cabins, dine on superb cuisine or simply sit back and take in the scenery as the train rushes on its elegant journey across Europe.

You'll be seeped in history just sitting on the train. Each carriage has been lovingly restored and has its own story to tell. One carriage was stuck in a snowdrift for 10 days in 1934, another was shot at during the Second World War and a third was used to transport European royalty!

As you sit together on the journey, take time to chat and take an interest in the countryside swishing past. You'll both be experiencing the life of luxury, where breakfast is brought to your table and meals are served on proper china. Make the train journey the holiday itself or extend it with a stay at a destination of your choice.

101

144

# FAMOUS

# floating

# CITY

# VENETIAN CHARM

They say Venice is for lovers and what better way to find out than to actually go there! Take a short break to Italy's famous floating city and you'll be seduced by its beauty and charm. Venice can be an expensive trip as it's a big tourist destination, so plan on some high spending.

Take your time to see the sights, incorporating a gondola ride along the canals at night. The city stretches across 100 small islands in the Venetian Lagoon, along the Adriatic sea. As well as its beauty, it is known for its glassware, so leave space in your suitcase for a few souvenirs.

Cross the famous Rialto Bridge to St. Mark's Square. Linger at a pavement café. Make sure you stay up to watch the sun set over the water, or take a walk in the early morning when the piazzas are swept and the fishermen bring in the morning's catch.

Don't forget to eat either! Venice is home to many of Italy's famous dishes, and there is plenty of emphasis on fish, as you might expect from such a watery location. Indulge your sweet tooth with a few zaeti, tiny local biscuits made from polenta flour.

When you take a gondola ride, you'll get a completely different view of the city. As you glide through the water, you'll be able to admire the fabulous Renaissance architecture that makes the place so incredibly romantic.

You can also take to the canals on the water-buses, which are bigger, cheaper and you still get to see loads. Be realistic though, Venice can get very crowded, especially in summer. If you're the sort who likes a bit of space, then choose autumn or spring.

# Ways to Say I Love You...

# OUTSIDE THE BOX

# HEART ATTACK

Don't worry, this is much nicer than it sounds. It's a great one to do if you don't live together or if they are out for the day. While they are gone, pop to a craft store and buy thick paper or craft foam in their favorite colors.

Cut out lots of hearts in different sizes and stick them on to lollipop sticks, or thin stakes used to train plants. Then off you go and 'attack' the house with hearts. Stick them all over the front garden, attach them to the front door, the stairs, even stand them in the plug hole in the bathroom.

Who can fail to smile when they find that they've been 'heart attacked' all over! This also works well for cars. If it's their birthday, decorate their car inside and out with paper hearts.

You can do this on a smaller scale too. If they have a rucksack, laptop case or handbag, cut out lots of smaller hearts and pop them inside. Make sure you remember even the smallest places like the inside of their purse where they keep their change.

Pop hearts in the pockets of their coat when they hang them in the closet, sneak hearts into the pocket of their jeans. Go wild and have fun. If you fancy a change from hearts, use something they're really fond of as a template.

nicer

THAN it

SOUNDS

# CREATIVE FASHION

Make your love public! Get a T-shirt printed telling the world what you love about them. Lots of T-shirt printing places will happily print one shirt for you. Think about what you want the shirt to say and when you want to wear it. You could get a huge size to wear as a nightshirt or go for a tight-fitting top to wear with jeans.

You can get their name emblazoned across the top or make it more cryptic by using a phrase that's only familiar to you two. If you don't want to go to the expense of having someone else print a T-shirt for you, then pop to a craft store and buy some fabric marker pens and purchase a couple of plain T-shirts. This way you can do a his and hers version and wear them together!

Before you start writing, map out what you want to say. Keep it brief. I Love You says it all! Use their name and decorate it with lots of stars and hearts. Don't forget to decorate the back too. Have a whale of a time drawing all the things on it that makes them special.

If you don't want to do a T-shirt, buy a fabric bag to decorate. That way they can even think about you when they are out shopping. You can treat the bag as a shopping list by writing down all both of your favourite foods.

Or go for star signs. Check out the appropriate motif for their star sign – a crab if it's Cancer, a ram if it's Aries and so on, then draw your own version. Find out what their star sign's main traits are supposed to be. Pick out the best ones and add them to the bag. Mark them in bullet points, for example, Mr. Aries: passionate, sporty, patient. Or, Miss Gemini: fun, loving, exciting.

# TREASURE HUNT

This can be as small or as grand as you want. You can arrange a treasure hunt in one room, across the house and garden or as far afield as you like. Give your treasure hunt a theme and think about it carefully. Is it linked to an event such as a birthday or is it just a fun and cryptic way to say I Love You?

The best way to approach it is to have a certain number of clues leading to a 'prize' at the end. Each clue has to link into the next and this is where the fun starts. For a giggle you can base the clues around your relationship.

For example, maybe your first clue will tell them to look for the cushion that is the same colour as the shirt you were wearing on your first date together. If they know their stuff, they'll head straight for the blue cushion, not the pink one!

You can make it as easy or as difficult as you like. Link the clues together. Use them to spell something out, such as a destination or a restaurant you plan to take them to. If you're looking for a romantic night of fun then keep the treasure hunt in the house and set things up so that all their favorite things are included.

You can make it a full day hunt, starting with a note next to a breakfast tray which leads them to the bathroom where you have prepared them a bath, and so on. Decide yourself what the reward will be. It doesn't have to be expensive, it could just be a cuddle on the sofa in front of their favorite TV programme, a homemade meal or something more exotic – it's up to you!

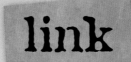

MAKE IT CRYPTIC

# HIDDEN TREATS

**D**ifferent from a treasure hunt in that there are no clues, just a great way to show them you love them in lots of different ways. Depending on how rich you're feeling, this can be a top-to-toe treats extravaganza, or a simple search for just one thing.

You can make it into a treat day or a treat hour. If you decide to go for the day, start bright and early. Set the table but leave the plates empty and pop a note on their plate telling them where to start looking. For instance, if they love pancakes, hide a jar of their favourite topping and leave them searching while you cook up the batter.

Move things on. If they like to relax with a DVD at the weekend, hint at where it might be hidden. Make it cryptic, if they love the Pirates of the Caribbean movies, draw a little picture of a pirate. Other things to hide include their shoes (to stop them going out so they can relax all day long).

The key here is to remember where you've hidden things, especially if they are perishable. For example, if you decide to make them search for their dessert and you've bought ice cream, it might be a better bet to leave a note in the hiding place that directs them to the freezer!

Adding notes for them to find extends the search and adds to the excitement. If you're feeling loved up, you could hide new nightclothes or underwear for them to find, letting them know what's in store later!

# MARATHON VIEWING

**D**o you like the same TV programmes? Probably not all of them, but it's a good bet that there will be some shows that you both love and couldn't imagine seeing without each other being there.

Set aside a day to indulge yourself in a whole nostalgic experience of your old favourites. Plan ahead and order them on DVD. If there are two or three shows you both love that aren't on TV any more, then get a selection to watch.

Book a day off work, or if the kids are at school, make sure you are incognito until pick-up time. Wear something comfortable and settle in for the duration. Make sure you've got plenty of appropriate snacks to hand throughout the day.

For instance, if you're both huge Simpsons fans, get some of the early series' and stock up on Homer's favourite doughnuts and a couple of beers, Springfield style.

If Sex and the City is your bag, snack on dainty cupcakes. The hit series is credited with starting the craze. You can make your own before you sit down or buy some ready-made colorful confections. Choose chocolate, or pink and white cakes swirled with icing.

settle in FOR THE DURATION

MOVIE

day to

REMEMBER

# MAGICAL MOVIES

Even if you've only been together a few months, you're bound to have been to the movies or watched a few DVDs together. If you've been together a long time, then you'll probably have a shared film history as long as your arm.

This is a great I Love You idea that you can both really enjoy. You can either choose to give them carte blanche and select four films of their choice. Or, you can sit down together and write down 10 favorites on separate strips of paper. Use two different colours, one for them, one for you. Then fold them up and pop them in a pot and draw two out each. There you have it, a movie day to remember.

You can be more specific if you like. If you fancy a sci-fi day or a roll of romantic comedies then make sure you only write those types of films down. Or, you could select a movie from every decade. For example, if romance is your thing you could pick Brief Encounter from the 1940s, High Society from the 1950s, Breakfast At Tiffany's from the 1960s and Love Story from the 1970s.

Make sure your movie snacks are in keeping with whatever you're watching. If it's romance, make it chocolates and cakes, even a glass of champagne. For sci-fi movies, go for a sugar high and grab some of your favorite childhood sweets.

Maybe your loved one is devoted to a particular actor or director. If she's mad for Harrison Ford, then make her day by surprising her with movie heaven in the shape of Blade Runner, Witness, Indiana Jones and Frantic. If Renée Zellweger gets him going, order in Bridget Jones' Diary, Chicago and Cold Mountain.

# HOT AIR BALLOON

First of all, make sure they like heights! Going up in a hot air balloon is one of the most beautiful and surprising gifts you can give someone. If you want to offer them a different view of the world, then this is a great way to do it. Wherever you are, a hot air balloon flight is breathtaking.

Whether you live in a city or in the country, the panoramic views from the air are amazing. Everything looks so different from way up high. The sight of your city from the air can be utterly fascinating and the peace of floating above rolling hills and woodland will live with them for a long time.

Because of the winds, many balloon flights happen early in the morning or just as the sun sets. Make sure you go for whichever time of day your partner love best. There are many reputable companies offering hot air balloon flights.

As you might expect, summer months are the most popular but the spring and autumn flights can offer fabulous views of the land as it springs into life after the winter, or as the colors change later on in the year.

Obviously you don't know exactly how long your flight will be or where you will land as that all depends on the winds. When you return to earth, many hot air balloon companies help you celebrate with a glass of bubbly!

*truly*

INDULGENT

experience

# AT HOME SPA DAY

A day at a spa is a lovely and truly indulgent experience, but most of us can only afford one every once in a while. What better way to say I Love You than to have your own spa at home. You can spend as much or as little as you like.

Make sure there's plenty of hot water and that the house is nice and warm. Lock the door, put the answer phone on and turn your mobiles off. Next, give each other a nice relaxing facial. Cleanse, exfoliate and apply a nice refreshing face mask. Pop on a couple of slices of cucumber on your eyelids and lie side by side, relaxing for 10 minutes.

Toss a coin to see who removes each other's face masks first. Or have fun by removing your masks at the same time. Splash lots of cool water on your faces to ensure that all the residue is removed, then pat dry and add a moisturiser to suit your skin type: normal, dry or combination.

The rest of the day is upto you. Spa days are all about rest and relaxation so make it what you want it to be. After the facial, you could both have showers and exfoliate with a refreshing body scrub, then moisturise with scented body lotion.

Pop on matching bathrobes and hit the kitchen for a light healthy snack of strawberries and delicious yoghurt. Or if you're having an indulgent spa day, eat lots of luxury fruit.

Spend the rest of the day catching up with each other. Chill out watching the TV programmes you've recorded and never got round to seeing, or finish that book you've been promising yourself. By the time you get back into the real world, you'll probably feel so relaxed it will look like you've been on holiday!

# STAR PERFORMANCE

**P**erfect for the star in your life! Lots of places offer the opportunity to name a star after someone you love. If this sounds like a random idea, then rest assured there are companies out there that have been helping people name stars for over 25 years.

Make sure you choose a reputable company. They will help you select a star that is visible with a telescope from where you live and give you the exact co-ordinates so that you can show your loved one just where it is.

To give astronomers a hand, the sky is divided into 88 zones called constellations. If you choose to name a star, reputable companies will tell you which is the best constellation to choose for optimum visibility.

One of the longest in the business is the International Star Registry. They offer stacks of advice and when you choose the star you also get a guide to the constellations and instructions on how to locate the star.

If you choose to name a star for someone's birthday then pick a star that is easily visible around their birthday time. There's no point naming a star that can be seen in June when their birthday is in January.

for THE star IN YOUR LIFE

RIG up your own

COSTUME

# KISSAGRAM FUN

It's not that long ago that professional kissagrams were the all the rage. You couldn't celebrate a birthday or anniversary without someone turning up in a gorilla suit or dressed like a fairy. The craze has gone now but why not surprise your loved one and get dressed yourself.

It's a brilliant way to say I Love You and doesn't need to cost the earth. You can rig up your own costume or opt to buy one. There are also plenty of fancy dress places that will hire them out for a reasonable cost.

So who will you be? It depends on what you want to say. Dress up as an ape and arrive on the doorstep asking them to monkey around with you. Wear a prince's outfit and tell them you're their knight in shining armour.

Pop on a fancy frock, grab a wand and tell them you're their fairy godmother and that you're here to grant them three wishes. Decide in advance if you want to attach any 'conditions' to those three wishes!

Perhaps you've booked them a ride in a racing car? Borrow someone's motorcycle helmet and leathers and deliver the news in style. If you're planning a holiday and you want to surprise them, then why not hire an airline pilot's costume and turn up at the front door with the tickets?

Don't feel like dressing up? Want to delegate the role to someone else? If you have a dog, buy a big fat ribbon and tie the message to its collar. No one can fail to be wooed by the sight of a waggly dog with a message under its chin!

# MEMORABLE TOKEN

This may seem like a cop-out. I mean, a gift card is just like a book token isn't it, for people who can't be bothered to choose a present? Actually, it's one of the things that people love most! Buying a gift card for their favourite shop is like giving them permission to choose whatever they like, without worrying about the money.

Virtually every shop, from supermarkets to clothes stores, sell gift cards these days. Think carefully about what they would like best. For the bookworm, it's like letting them loose in paradise for a couple of hours. A gift card for books means so many to choose from, so little time! And shoe-aholics will be in heaven if you get them a card. They can shop for heels without feeling the slightest bit of guilt.

Before you buy a card, check out the costs of the things they are likely to want to buy. Essentially you want them to be able to choose something they really want without feeling they have to top-up the card by using some of their own hard-earned cash.

Other places that offer gift cards are:

- Cinema: great for the movie buff.
- D.I.Y. shops: brilliant for the man who always has a project on the go.
- Restaurants: a must for anyone who likes good food.
- Beauty salons: a fabulous way to treat them to a makeover.

PERMISSION TO CHOOSE

A

*special*

TREAT

FOR both

# PAINT AND SHAVE

You have to trust people for this one. Depending on whether your mate is male or female, take charge and either help them shave or manicure their nails! This is a fun way to spend a few hours together and a special treat for both of you.

Shave

Make this a real treat. Buy him a new razor and some luxury shave gel. It might even be nice to invest in a new bottle of after shave. Settle him down in a comfortable chair and slather his face in shaving gel. Now concentrate!

Ask him for advice before you start and reassure him that you'll be very gentle and careful. Give him a smooth clean shave, help remove any excess gel and pat his face gently dry with a soft and fluffy towel. Splash on the new after shave. Perfect!

Manicure

Buy her some lovely hand cream and a couple of new shades of nail enamel. Soak her hands in warm water and dry. Massage cream into her hands and allow it to soak in. Remove any old nail enamel with cotton wool and nail enamel remover.

Depending on how elaborate you feel you can add a base coat before carefully painting each nail. Allow them to dry and then apply a second coat. For truly beautiful nails, finish off with a strengthening top coat.

# FEED THE DUCKS

This one will take you back to the days when you were little kids. Remember what brilliant fun it was to take a bag of old bread crusts and go down to the canal or the lake to feed the ducks. They'd squabble and bicker and peck each other in their hurry to get to the bread before anyone else.

Even if you have children, get someone else to watch them for a bit and pop out with your partner. Make it the focal point of a walk or a day out. Save up the old bread crusts from loaves for a few days to make it worthwhile.

This one is great at any time of year but particularly lovely in the winter and at the end of spring when all the babies hatch out. Make a point of going down to the water on a frosty day in winter and the ducks will really thank you.

The cold weather means food is scarce for them and tucking into a bit of bread can really make the difference and help them last through the cold spell. Depending on when you go, you're likely to see more than just ducks as swans and geese like to hang around too.

At the end of spring, the first ducklings appear and within days they've built up the confidence to be shown off by their proud parents. See if you can distract the greedy grown-ups so that the babies get some bread, too.

TIME

# NOVEL ROMANCE

One of the most romantic things you can do together is to read a romantic novel! Take it in turns to read to each other a chapter at a time. There are stacks to choose from, obviously, but one of the best books to read is one that you've read before and absolutely love. It's a wonderful way of introducing your lover to the things you like.

You can read to each other anywhere, at home or out and about. Try and make sure it's somewhere that you won't get disturbed. It takes time to read a good book so set aside an afternoon or evening every week to get through it.

If you're blessed with gorgeous weather, head for the park or garden and laze around reading. If it's cold out there, snuggle up together, in bed or on the sofa and get started on chapter one.

Romantic fiction is the obvious choice and a classic novel is even better. Here are some to choose from:

• Jane Eyre by Charlotte Brontë. The classic story of the plain governess who falls for the dark and mysterious Mr Rochester.
• Tess of the D'Urbervilles by Thomas Hardy. Beautiful country girl Tess gets seduced by the roguish Alec and falls for Angel Clare in this romantic tragedy.
• Pride and Prejudice by Jane Austen. The Bennet sisters search for love and marriage, helped and hindered by Mr Darcy.
• The Notebook by Nicholas Sparks. A lovely moving story about a man whose wife develops Alzheimer's, so he writes their love story in a notebook – the story she can't remember.

# BACK TO BASICS

**Y**ou may feel like you know each other inside out, but how long is it since you actually went out on a date? Not a quick nip to the fast food place, or a browse of the DVD rental place together but an actual date? Thought so! It's been a long time hasn't it? Well, now's the time to put that right and do it properly again.

Remember the first few dates. You thought carefully about where would be best to go. You spent ages wondering what to wear. You showered and came out scented and gorgeous. Well, do it again! Invite your partner on a date. Tell them what sort of place it will be and take it from there. It can be whatever you want it to be. Formal or informal, but make it special.

If there's a fancy new restaurant that has recently opened, invite them to join you there. Arrange to meet in a bar before and make sure you're on time. When they arrive, be polite and buy them a drink, then sit down and chat as if you've only just met. You'll probably even find that you're slightly nervous. That's because we all get nice and comfortable in our old ways and doing something different can reignite the spark.

Keep the compliments flowing. Be interested in what they have to say. Listen and offer some interesting little anecdotes yourself. And remember your manners! Let them order first and invite them to choose the wine. What matters most is that by pretending that you're on a date you rekindle some of the things that attracted you to your partner in the first place.

# Keep

## THE

### *compliments*

# flowing

YOUR

own

personal

DISPLAY

# EXPLOSIVE THRILLS

What a great way to say I Love You. For the person who makes the sparks fly in your life, give them their very own firework display. Even if it's not a national holiday, it's still fairly easy to purchase fireworks. Choose a few of their favourites.

Then 'invite' them to a firework party. Set everything up for the two of you. Prepare yummy firework food, hot dogs and hot soup. Buy or make toffee apples to get in the mood. You could even try your hand at making sweetmeats like fudge to keep up your energy levels and ward off the chills.

Wait until dark and then get started. Guide them into the garden and provide seating. Then tell them you love the fireworks in your relationship and you want to celebrate with your own personal display. Don't forget to buy sparklers, that way you can practise drawing hearts in sparks, or write their name in the sky.

If you can't manage to do your own fireworks, wait until you can take them to an organised display. Wrap up warm with hats and scarves. Buy them new gloves to stop them getting chilled to the bone and set off into the dark together. Cuddling up together as you watch the fireworks can be terrific fun and oohing and ahhing at the sight of rockets soaring across the sky will give you a nice warm feeling.

One big advantage of getting cold together is the fun you can have warming each other back up when you get home. In fact, it's almost worth getting chilly just to unwind together in front of a warm fire, reminiscing over which fireworks you liked best.

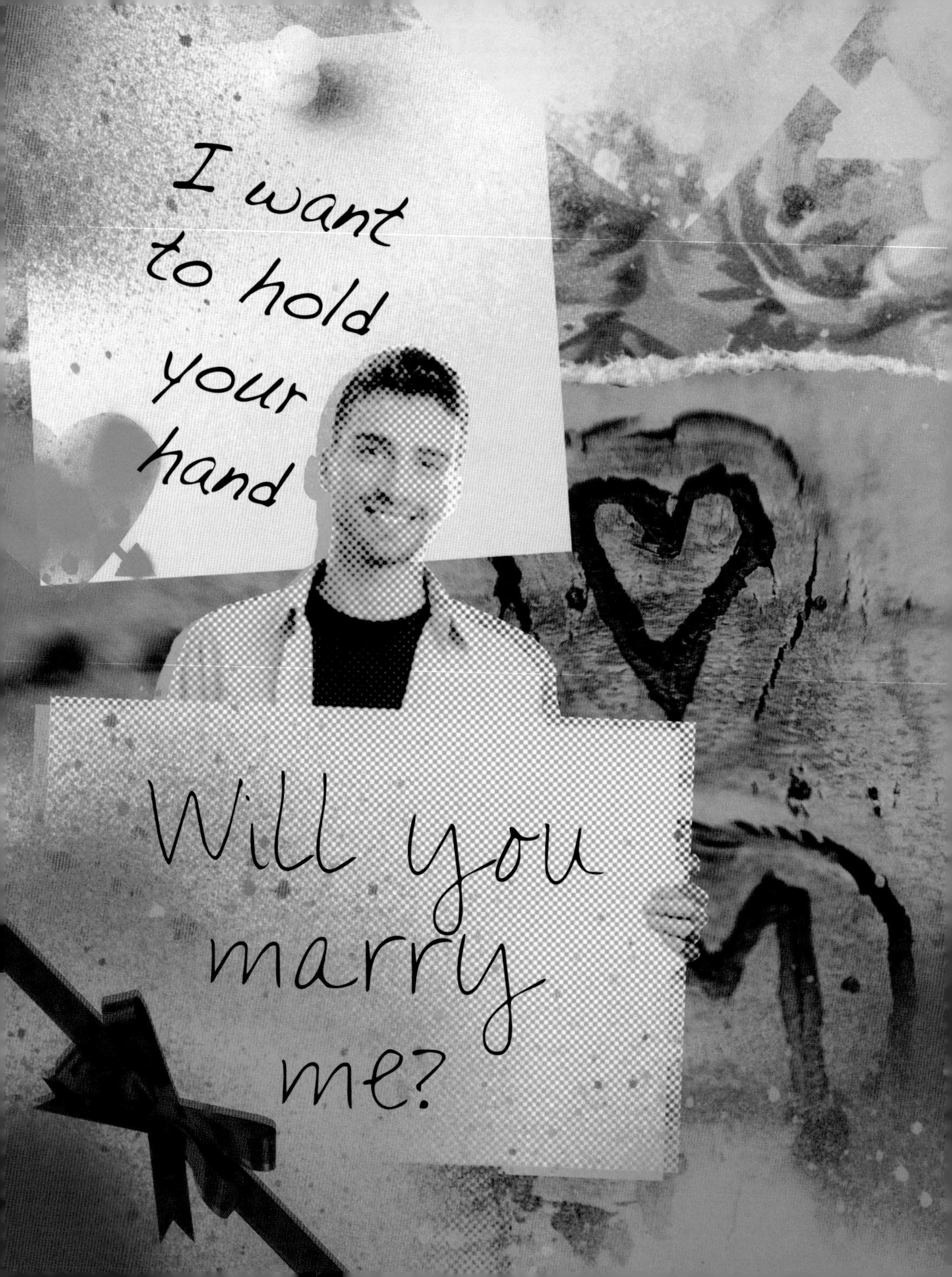
I want to hold your hand
Will you marry me?

# Ways to Say I Love You...
# ZERO COST

memory jar

# CARVE A SYMBOL

All the best movies and stories feature someone carving their initials into a tree. What could be better than entwining your initials in an announcement of how much you love each other? So how do you do it? Pick a tree, if you're worried about getting into trouble, do it on a tree in your own garden.

The main thing is that you don't want to damage the tree so just peel a small amount of bark off. You need a sharp knife to do it and plenty of patience. This might be a job that takes you a couple of days.

Carve a heart and then add your initials. Include a romantic arrow if you fancy. If you don't want to carve into a tree, then there are lots of other options.

You could get a piece of wood from a D.I.Y. store and do it that way. If the wood seems too tough, buy soft modelling wood like balsa wood. You only need a modelling knife to make a decent mark in that. That makes for a much more environmentally friendly way of declaring your love, too.

Another idea is to draw a tree and add your own 'carving', then take a photograph of it and get it framed. There are even online sites now that let you choose a tree from a virtual forest and carve your initials into it that way.

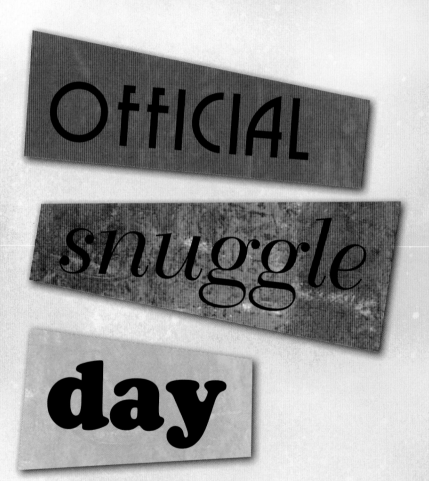

# GET SNUGGLING

A great one for the winter months when the temperatures have plummeted and you want to save money on heating bills. When it's cold outside and the radiators are on low, snuggle up close and keep warm.

Have an official snuggle day when you agree to do very little apart from keep close to your partner. You don't have to get all cheeky with them, unless you want to. In fact, sometimes keeping it to cuddles is even more sensual than hurling yourself at them.

So where to snuggle and what do you need? Comfortable clothes for a start. No one can have a snuggle in a suit and stilettos! Put your relaxing gear on or change into pyjamas and dressing gowns. Wear those fluffy indoor socks that show you're a real big softie.

The sofa is the ideal starting place for a serious snuggle. There's plenty of room for two and you can both stretch out if necessary. If you don't mind a squash you can squeeze into an armchair. Dedicated snugglers can create their own den. Bring a few duvets and pillows down, add a couple of fleece blankets and spread them all out into a cosy 'nest' on the floor.

You can even snuggle up when you're out and about. For this you'll need lots of layers of outdoor clothing, hats, gloves and scarves. Pick somewhere that you can watch the world go by. Good places include a sheltered park bench or a seafront shelter.

If you're going for outdoor snuggling, take sustenance with you. A flask of hot soup makes a welcome hand warmer when you both feel a little bit frosty. Not only will it warm you up, it will create happy memories for years to come!

# ROSE PETALS GALORE

An utterly romantic way to remind them how much you love them. You can use real rose petals or make your own from scraps of fabric or tissue paper. Buy lots of different colors and have fun cutting out your very own rose petal shapes. You can even make heart shapes for extra effect.

Treat the petals as a guide to what you want them to say. Remember the fairytale of Hansel and Gretel, where the children lay a trail of crumbs so they don't get lost in the forest? Of course, the birds eat the crumbs and the pair end up stuck at the nasty witch's house. If they'd laid a trail of petals they would have got back safely and anyone looking for them would have easily been able to find them.

That's the idea with petals. When your partner steps through the door they need to have an inkling of what's going on so they can work out what to do! Maybe you're feeling overwhelmingly romantic and fancy treating them to an afternoon of passion. Set a trail of petals up the stairs, all the way into the bedroom and even on to the covers. They'll get the message very quickly. You could even be under the covers yourself, ready and waiting…

Or maybe you know they've been snowed under at work and they've been fretting that the house is a mess and the kitchen cupboards are a nightmare. While they're out have a real blitz of the kitchen and chuck out all those jars and spices that are way past their sell by date. Then set a trail of petals through to the kitchen. Leave all the cupboard doors open to show just what you've done.

AN

AFTERNOON

OF

passion

# LEAVE

## subtle

# reminders

# SWEET AND SIMPLE

No time to talk? Rushed off your feet? Then get scribbling so that when you're out and about you're still talking to your loved one. Choose sticky notes or scraps of paper, you could even buy a pack of card in their favourite colour and cut it into heart shapes. Then leave a message, literally!

Leave a note under their pillow saying good night, even though you're lying next to them it will be a sweet reminder as they fall asleep. Try rolling up a note inside the towel they're taking swimming so that when they get dry they'll be reminded of how much you love them.

Are you living with a chocoholic or a cookie fan? Slip a note under the wrapper or in the cookie jar. You can even carve your love into some items. Draw a heart in the butter and then put the lid back on so that when they make their morning breakfast they get a wonderful surprise. Carve I Love You or hearts into the block of cheese.

You can also leave subtle reminders with your notes. For example, if he has a hopeless memory and you're due to go out that night, tell him you love him and remind him not to be late home. If she keeps promising to pick up the dry cleaning but keeps forgetting, give her a gentle nudge.

A polite reminder is easier to swallow when it's written inside a big heart and peppered with kisses. If you have children who also need gentle reminders once in a while, then adapt this one to use with them too.

# PLEASURE AND AMUSE

Get the games out and plan a day of fun. Twister, Operation, Connect 4, Cluedo, Monopoly, you name it, you play it. If you're the competitive type, this is the part you might struggle with. No matter how many times you play, this is the day that you're not afraid to lose a few times!

But, what if you've been brought up to win? What happens if you can't stop yourself hoarding hotels on Mayfair in Monopoly? Well, just for once you're going to have to get used to it and take a chance on the fact that you might lose.

Think of how nice it will be watching the smile on your loved one's face when they win. We're not suggesting you stop trying, just that you actually accept that sometimes, your loved one has better luck at games than you.

Switch off the TV, turn off the radio and concentrate! Among the games you should have in your arsenal are:

- Snakes and ladders: roll the dice and hope for ladders but don't despair if the snake drives you back to the bottom.
- Chess: so they've got you in check mate again. Admit defeat graciously, no tipping up the board in disgust.
- Card games: there are plenty that can be played with two players and many that can be spiced up, ever heard of strip poker?

MAKE

the effort

AND

WRITE IN

# RADIO REQUEST

**W**ith all the social networking sites around these days, the humble old radio show takes a bit of a back seat. Make the effort and write in for a request for your lover. Make sure you choose a show they listen to.

Many local radio shows are also more than happy to accept requests. Pick a show at a time they usually listen. Even though lots of stations offer a 'listen again' feature on the Internet, there's nothing quite like hearing your name read out live on the radio.

You can pick a birthday or an anniversary as a trigger, but a special event isn't essential. Sometimes we just want to say I Love You there and then, so get that request in and hope for the best. Listen ahead of sending in your missive and try to judge what requests get through.

Remember that hundreds of people write in to many of the big shows, so keep yours short and sweet. This may sound silly, but don't forget to include your name and theirs. So often people forget to say who the request is for. You can't get truly personal without including someone's first name.

And don't let your request fall flat by giving too much detail. If they hate people knowing how old they are then don't announce it to the world on the radio. Keep quiet! Likewise if you've planned a surprise party or meal, then don't announce it to the world first!

You could also ask the radio station to play your loved one's favorite song and ask them to dedicate it to them. If you want to make sure that they are definitely listening to the show, then send them a text message asking them to listen out for something special on the radio.

# CHORES WITH A SMILE

**D**o them without being asked! For many people, men and women, this is one of the best ways in the world of saying I Love You. Away from the hearts and flowers, the meals out and the fancy trips there is no better feeling than coming home to find that all the boring domestic stuff that clogs up our lives has been done!

If it's your partner who usually cleans the kitchen and carries out the rubbish then you do it for a change. If you normally have to be nagged to get the vacuum cleaner out, then whiz round and do it before they're back. Even better, do some of the jobs everyone hates, such as cleaning the toilets and emptying the dishwasher. If you're really on a charm offensive, then why not get those rubber gloves on and turn the oven from a greasy, smelly mess into a smart and shiny cooker!

Some of the outdoors jobs you choose to do will be noticed immediately. Get out there and mow the lawn while they're out. The scent of freshly mown grass is a giveaway but imagine the smile you'll spread across their face as they get out of their car and know the job's been done for them.

Sometimes, chores can seem so overwhelming that we leave them too long. If you spend some time putting that right, they'll love you for it. Finding simple ways to make someone else's day smoother shows them just how much they mean to you.

# WITHOUT being asked

# A NICE WARM GLOW

# LOVE HOLDING HANDS

That simple! When we first start dating, holding hands is something we do automatically, yet as we stay together longer it's something we can often neglect to do. Try taking your loved one's hand when walking down the street.

It's a great way to show your love and feel extra secure. Remind them how you feel about them when you next go for a meal. Reach over and take their hand across the table. Being in physical contact can help you feel closer emotionally.

Holding hands is even more important if you need to talk through a difficult issue or a problem. It's also a great demonstration of support if you're feeling down. Remember when you were little and your mum always held your hand tightly when you crossed the road?

Do you recall your dad grabbing your hot little palm as you walked through the big crowds together? It made you feel safe, didn't it? Safe and wanted and loved.

No matter how old you are, holding hands is a wonderful gesture. When you're out it shows that you are a couple and that you really care. If you ever see an elderly man and wife walking down the street together, it gives you a nice warm glow.

Next time you're walking the dog, slip your hand into theirs. When you're shopping together, take one hand off the trolley and entwine your fingers together. Don't be embarrassed, it shows the world how much you love them and it reminds your partner too.

# DRESSING UP GLAMOR

Be honest, are you sitting here in jeans reading this? Is your T-shirt so old that it's faded beyond belief? Last time you went out for a drink with the one you love, did you inwardly groan at the thought of putting on some footwear that wasn't sneakers?

In the early stages of your relationship you probably spent lots of time trying to look your best. You agonised over what top to wear, whether your shoes were too glam and spent forever checking if your earrings were too glitzy.

While it's nice to get to the stage where you're comfortable enough with each other to be happy in your lounge wear, it's nice now and again to rekindle things by getting dressed up. Make a pact with each other that every now and again you will glam up and really make an effort to look nice.

This means from top to toe, including your shoes, clothes, jewellery and make-up. No cutting corners allowed. If you have money to spare you can of course go to an up-market restaurant, but it's even more fun to get dressed up and sit down to a good meal at home.

One of the lovely things about getting dressed up is the pleasure you feel later on when you kick off your shoes and shrug off your jacket and relax. And who knows what that might lead to!

MAKE

A pact

WITH

EACH

other

# Plenty

## of eye

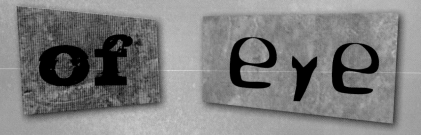

# CONTACT

# LISTENING IS KEY

Switch off your cell phone and leave the computer alone. It's all too easy for us to talk over people we love or find ourselves concentrating on what it says in the newspaper rather than actually listening. Let's be honest, we've all pretended to be listening without hearing a thing.

Sometimes, we're just too busy and preoccupied with our own thoughts. We're not listening, just going through the motions. So, to make their day, put down what you're doing, try to clear your mind of other stuff and listen.

Make a nice hot drink and invite them to sit down at the kitchen table. In soap operas, all the important chats go on in the kitchen, so copy their idea and talk. Ask them what they've been up to and really listen when they tell you.

Make plenty of eye contact as it really does show that you're listening and above all, that you care! Sometimes, it's not easy to start listening intently when you've got into the habit of really not taking much notice of what they are saying.

Gradually, you'll find they open up more and perhaps start to tell you things that have been bothering them. This can only be a good thing as unvoiced worries can lead to unnecessary stress in a relationship.

If you can get things out in the open it increases the trust and happiness in your love life. Often we forget to tell people things we should. Tell them that you're interested in what they have to say, ask their opinion and value their response. You'll both be glad you did.

# WORDS MATTER

**V**ery small words that make the world go round, or not. If you're frazzled and hassled it's easy to forget the things we were trained to do from a very early age. Most of us are pretty good at saying thank you but if you're run off your feet, sometimes the social niceties slip through the net and we end up sounding blunt and uncaring.

Even worse is that we do it to the people we love most and expect them to put up with it. Make sure you don't leave off the most important part of a sentence – the thank you. Make sure you mean it, too! Often, it can be an off-the-cuff add on that sounds shallow. Look at them when you say thank you, and smile.

The word please is another one that we tend to omit every now and again. We want our loved one to do something for us, to fetch our jacket from the car or to make a cup of coffee. Familiarity should mean we say please even more often as it lets people know that we really appreciate them and aren't just expecting things to happen without a little politeness.

Now for the big one – sorry. Like Elton John states in his song, sorry seems to be the hardest word. It's hard to accept that we are in the wrong or have put a foot out of place, actually admitting it out loud and in front of our lovers, is tough going. But remorse and apologies are part of life and learning to say sorry is all part of that. Your other half will appreciate you much more if you can hold your hands up and agree that you were wrong.

# MASSAGE PLEASURE

**H**ave you ever got home from work and felt like your shoulders were made from lead because of all the tension you're holding in? Chances are your partner often feels the same.

If they've been stuck behind the wheel for hours, hunched over a computer or standing up all day, they'll probably really appreciate a nice relaxing massage. First of all, run them a bath or a shower so they can soap away the grime of the day.

Offer them a nice cold beer or glass of wine, then get massaging. You don't need to be an expert to soothe away the soreness in their shoulders. Add a little scented oil or lotion to make the softness of your touch sink in quicker.

Work in broad, sweeping movements and keep things beautifully relaxed. Dim the lights and put on some soothing music, or just talk quietly about their day. If they do a job that involves lots of standing, such as teaching or working in a store, then offer to massage their calves and feet.

Pull up a chair and rest their legs on a towel in your lap, one at a time. Apply a little lotion and use soft circular movements to help relieve tension. When you've massaged both legs, rest their weary limbs on a silky cushion and leave them to relax.

Massage is a great way to remind them that you love them. It shows that you care about their physical wellbeing and it's a terrific way to reinforce physical and emotional closeness in your relationship.

# HUGS AND CUDDLES

**P**hysical gestures are very important in any relationship, particularly when you are partners. A hug can be just what they need to put a smile on their face. Develop a repertoire of hugs for different times and moods.

Sometimes a quick shrug of a hug can be all that's needed on a day when they have to go to work but just don't feel like it. It's a way of saying 'I know how you feel and I'm there for you' when talking might just spoil the moment.

Reserve your biggest hugs for welcomes and farewells. If they're going away on work-related business, make sure you give them a real bear hug so they know what they'll be missing while they're gone.

Are they trying something new and need reassurance? Put your arms around their shoulders and remind them you care. No words needed. Getting a hug makes them feel warm and cared for, and loved without question. You can create your own personal hugging style to use between the two of you.

Maybe you like to hug them round the waist and swing them round. Perhaps you're a shoulder squeezer, or maybe you like to bury your face in their chest and get up close that way. There is no right or wrong way to hug a loved one – just devise your own hugging rituals and remember this: hug often, hold on and keep it close!

PERSONAL

HUGGING

style

# SHARED

# experience

# GOES a

# LONG

# CULTURE DESIRES

One of the loveliest ways to say I Love You is to take a trip to a museum or art gallery and many of them are free to get into nowadays. Museums are fascinating places in their own right but when you take the one you love, you get to see things from a different perspective and learn a lot about the one you're with.

If you take a trip to the history museum, what do they head for first? The dinosaurs, the stuffed birds or the section that's crammed with lots of information about insects? Whichever it is doesn't really matter, but it can help you learn a lot more about their likes and dislikes.

Art galleries can be another eye opener. If you think you don't like art, then think again! Wandering round looking at paintings can be a fun thing to share, especially if you stop to talk about what you love and hate about each picture.

Take time to listen to what their favorites are and even if you struggle to appreciate paintings like they do, ask their advice about the work of great artists. Shared experience goes a long way and you can have a laugh about it too.

Places like museums and galleries are terrific for people watching; as you sit on a bench eating your packed lunch you can observe the way others make their way round the displays on show and giggle about it!

Don't forget to pick up an exhibition leaflet. More often than not, they are free of charge and will serve as a great reminder of the wonderful day you've spent together.

# NICE AND ICY

It's freezing cold outside, the car is iced up and the drive looks like a Christmas card, all snowy and crisp. The trouble is, your loved one has to get to work. You could stay under the covers in the nice warmth of the bed, or slip on a coat and some boots and really show them that you love them.

Get out that shovel and start digging. No one likes clearing their drive, but it has to be done. If they are usually the ones who do it, show your colors and save them a job. They'll love you for it. Shift the snow to the side so that they can back the car out and then carefully clear the windscreen and windows.

If you like, draw a snowy heart on the bonnet with a big kiss to remind them how wonderful they are. It all looks lovely when the snow and frost is hanging off branches and making the place look like a picture postcard. But it's not very nice when you've got to get in the car and drive somewhere.

Here's the plan to really show you love them. Leave them in bed and get yourself dressed into something warm. Wake them up gently with a nice warm drink. Then, while they are adjusting to the start of a new day, go out and sort their car for them.

Clear the windscreen and switch on the ignition to get the car warmed up. Make sure they have perfect visibility and a nice warm car, all achieved in the space of time it takes them to sip a hot drink!

# SQUEAKY CLEAN

It's a job we all hate doing and it's easy to let our cars get grimy and dirty without doing anything about it. You can put it through a car wash, yes, but think how happy they will be if they come home to find their car, gleaming and shiny on the drive, all thanks to you.

Do it properly by rinsing off all the surface grime with a hose and then froth the car all over with a big squashy sponge. Rinse it off, dry it and then wax it to a high shine until you can see your reflection in it.

Now for the interior. Every now and then we might throw away food packets that are festering in the glove box or fizzy drink bottles that are lolling in the footwell. But giving the car a really good clear out takes time and can be pretty hard work.

Vacuum the carpets for starters, and use a crevice tool to get into all the awkward corners. Vacuum the seats as well, if you're one of those people who eats on the run, then no doubt there will be dozens of crumbs down the backs of the seats.

Next, polish the dashboard, dust the dials and make sure those windows are spruced up to a perfect shine. Tidy up their CD collection and put it in order: alphabetical or by genre.

Make sure all the discs are in the right boxes so that when they get out Eminem they don't end up playing Michael Jackson! Then stock the glove box with driving essentials, including tissues, a pen, a packet of chewing gum and some coins for parking meters. They'll be over the moon!

# DREAM GARDEN

If this sounds like hard work, then don't let it be. You may have half an acre, a small patch or just a few pots on a balcony. Whatever it is, do it together. Getting green fingered as a couple can be a scream. It doesn't matter if you're hopeless or a horticultural genius, you can really make some progress.

If you're normally both quite single-minded, or if they're bossy and you're passive, gardening helps change that as it literally becomes a level playing field. Decide what you're going to do in the garden.

Weed, dig or plant new stuff. Don't try and do all three at once. Maybe it's time to tidy the garden ready for winter, so choose a weekend when you are both around to rake up the leaves and do any necessary pruning.

Of course, while you're raking them into a pile, you might just be tempted to pick up a handful and hurl them at your partner for a laugh. Who knows where that might lead!

If you decide to get gardening in the spring then it's all about preparation. Dust off the spade and the forks and work side by side clearing the ground and digging it through. Pick out all the weeds that are driving you crazy. To keep it exciting and less mundane, you could plan a few weekends of gardening and undertake different tasks each week. Devise a plan and stick to it.

A level playing FIELD

# Wander

## through

# countryside

# TAKE A HIKE

There's lots of fresh air out there and it's all free. Wherever you live, you won't be far from walking countryside. Even if you live in the city, there are plenty of canal sidewalks you can take with your honey.

And if all the land near you appears to be farmers' fields, there are often official footpaths running through them. Depending on where you walk, be prepared. You can't hike up a steep hill in a pair of flip-flops or wander through countryside in stilettos.

Check the weather before you go and make sure you are wearing the right clothes. If you're thinking of heading for the heights and up hill, be sure to pack an extra layer to allow for a chilly summit. Before you set off, decide how far you want to walk.

If you've not been hiking for a while, be sensible and start small. Allow lots of time, there's nothing worse than having a great day of hiking and then having to speed up on the last section because you're worried the gates to the car park will have been closed by the time you get back.

Pack yourself plenty of nutritious snacks, a picnic to share and stock up on drinks. Plan the route before you go and get a detailed map that shows you the paths.

Walking in the fresh air can give you a whole new lease of life and as you walk, you'll find yourself talking to your lover in a completely different way. Hiking can give you a real appetite, not just for food!

# BREAKFAST IN BED

There's no greater way to feel pampered and to set you up for the day than the delicious delights of breakfast in bed. Don't reserve it for birithdays or anniversaries, get creative and do it now! Pick a day when no one has to rush off anywhere. Leave them sleeping soundly and tiptoe downstairs.

Don't go the whole hog straight away. No one wants to be confronted by a massive pile of food first thing. Instead, make the drink they love most, either tea, coffee or fresh juice and take it upstairs. Make an event of it, pop it on a tray with a flower in a vase.

Kiss them gently until they wake up, leave the drink on the bedside table and sneak off. Leave them time to become fully awake. Pop downstairs and have a drink yourself while planning your next move. Are you going to cook a hot breakfast, go continental, or do your own thing? Have a really good think about what would go down best.

For instance, if it's a chilly winter day then a warming bowl of porridge with maple syrup might be perfect. Or get out the bacon and sizzle up a sandwich. If it's warm and summery go for fresh fruit salad followed by a croissant warmed up in the oven for maximum tastiness. You know your partner best!

Set a new tray with all the bits and pieces they'll need, including butter, spreads and sauces. Don't forget the little extras make all the difference. And when you're done, remember to wash the dishes. That really will make their day!

MAKE an EVENT of it

# SHOUT IT from THE ROOFTOPS

# SAY IT AND MEAN IT

Has anyone ever said I Love You and not meant it? Go on, be honest with yourself, of course we have. A cursory I Love You, or even 'me too' when they declare their love, can be a lazy daisy way of getting away with basic niceties.

Come on everyone, shout it from the rooftops. Say I Love You and really mean it, all the way down to your toes. It really makes their day. Imagine she's got a long day ahead. Just before she steps out of the door pull her back, put on your most serious face, look straight into her eyes and tell her that you really truly love her.

It's not a cliché to really take time to remind the person you're with that you really care about them. When he's busy at work, pick a time when you know he'll have a couple of minutes to give him a call and remind him. Again, make it clear and be sincere.

Those three little words can trip off the tongue and get us off the hook at the worst of times. Own up to your love when you've done something wrong, don't just say I Love You in the hope they'll let you off. Use the occasion to really show them.

Even when things are going really well, it can be easy to forget to declare our love. Actually, sometimes all idea of admitting it goes out of the window. It's as if we're scared that by saying I Love You, we will curse the relationship.

Well, stop being so superstitious, take one long deep breath and yell: I LOVE YOU for the world to hear. Worried about being embarrassing? Don't, the world loves a pair of lovers, and who knows, it could be infectious!